# How Will
# You Measure
# Your Life?

# HOW WILL
# YOU MEASURE
# YOUR LIFE?

~

## CLAYTON M. CHRISTENSEN,

### James Allworth, and Karen Dillon

**HARPER**
BUSINESS

*An Imprint of* HarperCollins*Publishers*
www.harpercollins.com

HOW WILL YOU MEASURE YOUR LIFE? Copyright © 2012 by Clayton M. Christensen, James Allworth, and Karen Dillon. All rights reserved. Printed in the United States of America. No part of this book may be used or reproduced in any manner whatsoever without written permission except in the case of brief quotations embodied in critical articles and reviews. For information, address HarperCollins Publishers, 10 East 53rd Street, New York, NY 10022.

HarperCollins books may be purchased for educational, business, or sales promotional use. For information, please write: Special Markets Department, HarperCollins Publishers, 10 East 53rd Street, New York, NY 10022.

*Designed by Katy Riegel*

Library of Congress Cataloging-in-Publication Data has been applied for.

ISBN 978-0-06-210241-6 (hardcover)
ISBN 978-0-06-220619-0 (international edition)

12 13 14 15 16    OV/RRD    10 9 8 7 6

# CONTENTS

~

# Contents

*To our families*

~

# How Will
# You Measure
# Your Life?

# PROLOGUE

~

ON THE LAST day of the course that I teach at Harvard Business School, I typically start by telling my students what I observed among my own business school classmates after we graduated. Just like every other school, our reunions every five years provided a series of fascinating snapshots. The school is superb at luring back its alumni for these events, which are key fund-raisers; the red carpet gets rolled out with an array of high-profile speakers and events. My own fifth-year reunion was no exception and we had a big turnout. Looking around, everyone seemed so polished and prosperous—we couldn't help but feel that we really were part of something special.

We clearly had much to celebrate. My classmates seemed to be doing extremely well; they had great jobs, some were working in exotic locations, and most had managed to marry spouses much better-looking than they were. Their lives seemed destined to be fantastic on every level.

But by our tenth reunion, things that we had never expected became increasingly common. A number of my classmates whom I had been looking forward to seeing didn't come back, and I had no idea why. Gradually, by calling them or asking other friends, I put the pieces together. Among my classmates were executives at renowned consulting and finance firms like McKinsey & Co. and Goldman Sachs; others were on their way to top spots in Fortune 500 companies; some were already successful entrepreneurs, and a few were earning enormous, life-changing amounts of money.

Despite such professional accomplishments, however, many of them were clearly unhappy.

Behind the facade of professional success, there were many who did not enjoy what they were doing for a living. There were, also, numerous stories of divorces or unhappy marriages. I remember one classmate who hadn't talked to his children in years, who was now living on the opposite coast from them. Another was on her third marriage since we'd graduated.

My classmates were not only some of the brightest people I've known, but some of the most decent people, too. At graduation they had plans and visions for what they would accomplish, not just in their careers, but in their personal lives as well. Yet something had gone wrong for some of them along the way: their personal relationships had begun to deteriorate, even as their professional prospects blossomed. I sensed that they felt embarrassed to explain to their friends the contrast in the trajectories of their personal and professional lives.

At the time, I assumed it was a blip; a kind of midlife crisis. But at our twenty-five- and thirty-year reunions, the problems were worse. One of our classmates—Jeffrey Skilling—had landed in jail for his role in the Enron scandal.

The Jeffrey Skilling I knew of from our years at HBS was a good man. He was smart, he worked hard, he loved his family. He had been one of the youngest partners in McKinsey & Co.'s history and later went on to earn more than $100 million in a single year as Enron's CEO. But simultaneously, his private life was not as successful: his first marriage ended in divorce. I certainly didn't recognize the finance shark depicted in the media as he became increasingly prominent. And yet when his entire career unraveled with his conviction on multiple federal felony charges relating to Enron's financial collapse, it not only shocked me that he had gone wrong, but how spectacularly he had done so. Something had clearly sent him off in the wrong direction.

Personal dissatisfaction, family failures, professional struggles, even criminal behavior—these problems weren't limited to my classmates at HBS. I saw the same thing happen to my classmates in the years after we completed our studies as Rhodes Scholars at Oxford University. To be given that opportunity, my classmates had to have demonstrated extraordinary academic excellence; superior performance in extracurricular activities such as sports, politics, or writing; and significant contributions to their communities. These were well-rounded, accomplished people who clearly had much to offer the world.

But as the years went by, some of my thirty-two Rhodes classmates also experienced similar disappointments. One played a prominent role in a major insider trading scandal, as recounted in the book *Den of Thieves*. Another ended up in jail because of a sexual relationship with a teenager who had worked on his political campaign. He was married with three children at the time. One who I thought was destined for greatness in his professional and family spheres has struggled in both—including more than one divorce.

I know for sure that none of these people graduated with a deliberate strategy to get divorced or lose touch with their children—much less to end up in jail. Yet this is the exact strategy that too many ended up implementing.

I don't want to mislead you. Alongside these disappointments, there are many of my classmates who have led exemplary personal lives; they have truly been an inspiration to me. But our lives are not over, and the lives of our children are just now unfolding. Understanding what causes the problems that trapped some of my classmates is important not just for those who have come off the path that they had planned to follow but for those whose lives are still on the right path—as well as those whose journeys are just beginning. We all are vulnerable to the forces and decisions that have derailed too many.

I am among those who have been fortunate so far—in many ways due to my wonderful wife, Christine, who has helped us see into the future with remarkable prescience. It would be folly for me to write this book, however, to proclaim that everyone who replicates the decisions we have made will be happy and successful, too. Instead, in writing this book, I have followed the approach that has characterized my management research.

I have engaged my students in the quest as well. In my MBA course, Building and Sustaining a Successful Enterprise, we study theories regarding the various dimensions of the job of general managers. These theories are statements of what *causes* things to happen—and why. When the students understand these theories, we put them "on"—like a set of lenses—to examine a case about a company. We discuss what each of the theories can tell us about why and how the problems and opportunities emerged in the company. We then use the theories to predict what problems and opportunities are likely to occur in the future for that company, and we use the theories to predict what actions the managers will need to take to address them.

By doing this, the students learn that a robust theory is able to explain what has and what will occur across the hierarchy of business: in industries; in the corporations within those industries; in the business units within those corporations; and in the teams that are within the business units.

In the past several years, on the last day of my class after I've summarized what so frequently happens in the lives of our graduates, we have taken the discussion a step further, plumbing to the most fundamental element of organizations: individuals. For this discussion, rather than use businesses as the case studies, we use ourselves.

I participate in these discussions with more history than my students do, but I follow the same rules. We are there to explore not what we *hope* will happen to us but rather what the theories *predict* will happen to us, as a result of different decisions and actions. Because I've been present in these discussions over many years, I've learned more about these issues than any one group of my students ever has. To even the score with them, however, I have shared stories about how these theories have played out in my life.

To help structure this discussion, I write the theories we have studied along the top of the chalkboard. Then I write three simple questions beside those theories:

*How can I be sure that*

- *I will be successful and happy in my career?*
- *My relationships with my spouse, my children, and my extended family and close friends become an enduring source of happiness?*
- *I live a life of integrity—and stay out of jail?*

These questions might sound simple, but they are questions that so many of my classmates never asked, or had asked but lost track of what they learned.

Year after year I have been stunned at how the theories of the course illuminate issues in our personal lives as they do in the companies we've studied. In this book, I will try to summarize some of the best of the insights my students and I have discussed on that last day in class.

\* \* \*

IN THE SPRING of 2010, I was asked to speak not just to the students in my own class but to the entire graduating student body. But that's not the only way things were a little different that day. Standing at the podium with little hair as the result of chemotherapy, I explained that I had been diagnosed with follicular lymphoma, a cancer similar to that which had killed my father. I expressed my gratitude that I could use this time with them to summarize what my students and I had learned from focusing these theories on ourselves. I spoke about the things in our lives that are most important—not just when you are confronting a life-threatening illness, as I was, but every day, for every one of us. Sharing my thoughts that day with the students about to make their own way in the world was a remarkable experience.

James Allworth, who was in my class that semester and in the audience that day, and Karen Dillon, who heard about my remarks in her position as editor of the *Harvard Business Review*, were both extremely moved by the topic. I later asked them to help me convey to a broader audience the feeling people had that day in Burden Hall on the Harvard Business School campus.

We are from three different generations and have completely different beliefs informing our lives. James is a recent business school graduate, who assures me that he is an atheist. I'm a father and grandfather with a deeply held faith, far into my third professional career. Karen, the mother of two daughters, is two decades into a career as an editor. She says her beliefs and career fall someplace between us.

But the three of us are united in the goal of helping you understand the theories we share in this book because we believe they can sharpen the acuity with which you can examine and improve your life. We've written in the first person, my voice, because it's how I talk to my students—and my own children—about this thinking. But James and Karen have truly been coauthors in deed.

I don't promise this book will offer you any easy answers: working through these questions requires hard work. It has taken me decades. But it has also been one of the most worthwhile endeavors of my life. I hope the theories in this book can help you as you continue on your journey, so that in the end, you can definitively answer for yourself the question "How will you measure your life?"

# CHAPTER ONE

## *Just Because You Have Feathers . . .*

*There are probably dozens of well-intended people who have advice for how you should live your life, make your career choices, or make yourself happy. Similarly, walk into the self-help section of any bookstore and you'll be overwhelmed with scores of choices about how you can improve your life. You know, intuitively, that all these books can't be right. But how can you tell them apart? How do you know what is good advice—and what is bad?*

~

### The Difference Between What to Think and How to Think

There are no easy answers to life's challenges. The quest to find happiness and meaning in life is not new. Humans have been pondering the reason for our existence for thousands of years.

What is new, however, is how some modern thinkers address the problem. A bevy of so-called experts simply offer the answers. It's not a surprise that these answers are very appealing to some. They take hard problems—ones that people can go through an entire life without ever resolving—and offer a quick fix.

That is not what I intend with this book. There are no quick fixes for the fundamental problems of life. But I can offer you tools that I'll call *theories* in this book, which will help you make good choices, appropriate to the circumstances of your life.

I learned about the power of this approach in 1997, before I published my first book, *The Innovator's Dilemma*. I got a call from Andy Grove, then the chairman of Intel. He had heard of one of my early academic papers about disruptive innovation, and asked me to come to Santa Clara to explain my research and tell him and his top team what it implied for Intel. A young professor, I excitedly flew to Silicon Valley and showed up at the appointed time, only to have Andy say, "Look, stuff has happened. We have only ten minutes for you. Tell us what your research means for Intel, so we can get on with things."

I responded, "Andy, I can't, because I know very little about Intel. The only thing I can do is to explain the theory first; then we can look at the company through the lens that the theory offers." I then showed him a diagram of my theory of disruption. I explained that disruption happens when a competitor enters a market with a low-priced product or service that most established industry players view as inferior. But the new competitor uses technology and its business model to continually improve its offering until it is good enough to satisfy what customers need. Ten minutes into my explanation, Andy interrupted impatiently: "Look, I've got your model. Just tell us what it means for Intel."

I said, "Andy, I still can't. I need to describe how this process worked its way through a very different industry, so you can visualize how it works." I told the story of the steel-mill industry, in which Nucor and other steel mini-mills disrupted the integrated steel-mill giants. The mini-mills began by attacking at the lowest end of the market—steel reinforcing bar, or rebar—and then step by step moved up toward the high end, to make sheet steel—eventually driving all but one of the traditional steel mills into bankruptcy.

When I finished the mini-mill story, Andy said, "I get it. What it means for Intel is . . ." and then went on to articulate what would become the company's strategy for going to the bottom of the market to launch the lower-priced Celeron processor.

I've thought about that exchange a million times since. If I had tried to tell Andy Grove what he should think about the microprocessor business, he would have eviscerated my argument. He's forgotten more than I will ever know about his business.

But instead of telling him *what* to think, I taught him *how* to think. He then reached a bold decision about what to do, on his own.

## I Don't Have an Opinion, the *Theory* Has an Opinion

That meeting with Andy changed the way I answer questions. When people ask me something, I now rarely answer directly. Instead, I run the question through a theory in my own mind, so I know what the theory says is likely to be the result of one course of action, compared to another. I'll then explain how it applies to their question. To be sure they understand it, I'll describe to them how the process in the model worked its way through an industry or situation different from their own, to help them visualize how it works. People, typically, then say, "Okay, I get it." They'll then answer their question with more insight than I could possibly have.

A good theory doesn't change its mind: it doesn't apply only to some companies or people, and not to others. It is a general statement of what causes what, and why. To illustrate, about a year after meeting with Andy Grove, I received a call from William Cohen, then–secretary of defense in the Clinton administration. He told me he'd read *The Innovator's Dilemma*. "Could you come to Washington and talk to me and my staff about your research?" he asked. To me, this was a once-in-a-lifetime opportunity.

When Secretary Cohen had said "my staff," somehow I had imagined second lieutenants and college interns. But when I walked into the secretary's conference room, the Joint Chiefs of Staff were in the front row, followed by the secretaries of the Army, Navy, and Air Force, and then each of the secretaries' under-, deputy, and assistant secretaries. I was stunned. He said that this was the first time he had convened all of his direct reports in one room.

Secretary Cohen simply asked me to present my research. So using the exact same PowerPoint slides I had used with Andy Grove, I started explaining the theory of disruption. As soon as I had explained how the mini-mills had undermined the traditional steel industry by starting with rebar at the bottom, General Hugh Shelton, then the chairman of the Joint Chiefs of Staff, stopped me. "You have no idea why we are interested in this, do you?" he queried. Then he gestured to the mini-mill chart. "You see the sheet steel products at the top of the market?" he asked. "That was the Soviets, and they're not the enemy anymore." Then he pointed to the bottom of the market—rebar—and said, "The rebar of our world is local policing actions and terrorism." Just as the mini-mills had attacked the massive integrated mills at the bottom of the market and then moved up, he worried aloud, "Everything about the way we do our jobs is focused on the high end of the problem—what the USSR used to be."

Once I understood why I was there, we were able to discuss what the result of fighting terrorism from within the existing departments would be, versus setting up a completely new organization. The Joint Chiefs later decided to go down the route of forming a new entity, the Joint Forces Command, in Norfolk, Virginia. For more than a decade, this command served as a "transformation laboratory" for the United States military to develop and deploy strategies to combat terrorism around the world.

On the surface, competition in the computer chip market and the proliferation of global terrorism could not seem like more different problems to tackle. But they are fundamentally the same problem, just in different contexts. Good theory can help us categorize, explain, and, most important, predict.

People often think that the best way to predict the future is by collecting as much data as possible before making a decision. But this is like driving a car looking only at the rearview mirror—because data is only available about the past.

Indeed, while experiences and information can be good teachers, there are many times in life where we simply cannot afford to learn on the job. You don't want to have to go through multiple marriages to learn how to be a good spouse. Or wait until your last child has grown to master parenthood. This is why theory can be so valuable: it can explain what will happen, even before you experience it.

Consider, for example, the history of mankind's attempts to fly. Early researchers observed strong correlations between being able to fly and having feathers and wings. Stories of men attempting to fly by strapping on wings date back hundreds of years. They were replicating what they believed allowed birds to soar: wings and feathers.

Possessing these attributes had a high *correlation*—a connection between two things—with the ability to fly, but when humans attempted to follow what they believed were "best practices" of the most successful fliers by strapping on wings, then jumping off cathedrals and flapping hard . . . they failed. The mistake was that although feathers and wings were correlated with flying, the would-be aviators did not understand the fundamental *causal mechanism*—what actually causes something to happen—that enabled certain creatures to fly.

The real breakthrough in human flight didn't come from crafting better wings or using more feathers. It was brought about by Dutch-Swiss mathematician Daniel Bernoulli and his book *Hydrodynamica*, a study of fluid mechanics. In 1738, he outlined what was to become known as Bernoulli's principle, a theory that, when applied to flight, explained the concept of lift. We had gone from correlation (wings and feathers) to causality (lift). Modern flight can be traced directly back to the development and adoption of this theory.

But even the breakthrough understanding of the cause of flight still wasn't enough to make flight perfectly *reliable*. When an airplane crashed, researchers then had to ask, "What was it about the circumstances of that particular attempt to fly that led to failure? Wind? Fog? The angle of the aircraft?" Researchers could then define what rules pilots needed to follow in order to succeed in each different circumstance. That's a hallmark of good theory: it dispenses its advice in "if-then" statements.

## The Power of Theory in Our Lives

How do fundamental theories relate to finding happiness in life?

The appeal of easy answers—of strapping on wings and feathers—is incredibly alluring. Whether these answers come from writers who are hawking guaranteed steps for making millions, or the four things you have to do to be happy in marriage, we want to believe they will work. But so much of what's become popular thinking isn't grounded in anything more than a series of anecdotes. Solving the challenges in your life requires a deep understanding of what causes what to happen. The theories that I will discuss with you will help you do exactly that.

This book uses research done at the Harvard Business School and in some of the world's other leading universities. It has been rigorously tested in organizations of all sizes around the world.

Just as these theories have explained behavior in a wide range of circumstances, so, too, do they apply across a wide range of questions. With most complex problems it's rarely as simple as identifying the one and only theory that helps solve the problem. There can be multiple theories that provide insight. For example, though Bernoulli's thinking was a significant breakthrough, it took other work—such as understanding gravity and resistance—to fully explain flight.

Each chapter of this book highlights a theory as it might apply to a particular challenge. But just as was true in understanding flight, problems in our lives don't always map neatly to theories on a one-to-one basis. The way I've paired the challenges and theories in the subsequent chapters is based on how my students and I have discussed them in class. I invite you, as you journey through the book, to go back to theories in earlier chapters, just as my students do, and explore the problems through the perspective of multiple theories, too.

These theories are powerful tools. I have applied many of them in my own life; others I wish I'd had available to me when I was younger, struggling with a problem. You'll see that without theory, we're at sea without a sextant. If we can't see beyond what's close by, we're relying on chance—on the currents of life—to guide us. Good theory helps people steer to good decisions—not just in business, but in life, too.

~

*You might be tempted to try to make decisions in your life based on what you know has happened in the past or what has happened to other people. You should learn all that you can from the past; from scholars who have studied it, and from people who have gone through problems of the sort that you are likely to face. But this doesn't solve the fundamental challenge of what information and what advice you should accept, and which you should ignore as you embark into the future. Instead, using robust theory to predict what will happen has a much greater chance of success. The theories in this book are based on a deep understanding of human endeavor—what causes what to happen, and why. They've been rigorously examined and used in organizations all over the globe, and can help all of us with decisions that we make every day in our lives, too.*

# SECTION I

~

## *Finding Happiness in Your Career*

The only way to be truly satisfied is to do what you believe is great work. And the only way to do great work is to love what you do. If you haven't found it yet, keep looking. Don't settle. As with all matters of the heart, you'll know when you find it.

—*Steve Jobs*

WHEN YOU WERE ten years old and someone asked you what you wanted to be when you grew up, anything seemed possible. Astronaut. Archaeologist. Fireman. Baseball player. The first female president of the United States. Your answers then were guided simply by what you thought would make you really happy. There were no limits.

There are a determined few who never lose sight of aspiring to do something that's truly meaningful to them. But for many of us, as the years go by, we allow our dreams to be peeled away. We pick our jobs for the wrong reasons and then we settle for them. We begin to accept that it's not realistic to do something we truly love for a living.

Too many of us who start down the path of compromise will never make it back. Considering the fact that you'll likely spend more of your waking hours at your job than in any other part of your life, it's a compromise that will always eat away at you.

But you need not resign yourself to this fate.

I had been out of college and in the working world for years before I figured out that I could make it back to school to teach and develop a generation of wonderful young people. For a long time, I had no idea that this might be possible. Now there's nothing I would rather be doing. Every day I think of how fortunate I am.

I want you to be able to experience that feeling—to wake up every morning thinking how lucky you are to be doing what *you're* doing. Together, in the next chapters, we're going to build a strategy for you to do exactly that.

A strategy? At a basic level, a strategy is what you want to achieve and how you will get there. In the business world, this is the result of multiple influences: what a company's priorities are, how a company responds to opportunities and threats along the way, and how a company allocates its precious resources. These things all continuously combine, to create and evolve a strategy.

You don't need to think about this for more than a minute, however, before you realize that this same strategy-making process is at work in every one of us as well. We have intentions for our careers. Against those intentions, opportunities and threats emerge that we haven't anticipated. And how we allocate our resources—our time, talent, and energies—is how we determine the actual strategy of our lives. Occasionally, the actual strategy maps quite closely with what we intended. But often what we actually end up doing is very different from what we set out to do.

The art of managing this, however, is not to simply stomp out anything that was not a part of the original plan. Among those threats and opportunities that we didn't anticipate, there are almost always better options than were contained in our original plans. The strategist in us needs to figure out what these better things are, and then manage our resources in order to nourish them.

The following chapters are all designed to help you leverage these concepts in answering the question "How can I find happiness in my career?"

The starting point for our journey is a discussion of priorities. These are, in effect, your core decision-making criteria: what's most important to you in your career? The problem is that what we think matters most in our jobs often does not align with what will really make us happy. Even worse, we don't notice that gap until it's too late. To help you avoid this mistake, I want to discuss the best research we have on what truly motivates people.

Following this, I will outline how best to balance our plans to find something that we truly love doing with the opportunities and challenges that we never expected to arise in our lives. While some people will argue that you should always have the next five years of your life planned out, others have followed a strategy of just seeing what has come along and will tell you that it's worked well for them. There's a time and a place for both approaches. Drawing on our research, I will explain what the best circumstances are to be deliberate, to have that plan; and when it's best to be emergent—to be open to the unexpected.

The final element is execution. The only way a strategy can get implemented is if we dedicate resources to it. Good intentions are not enough—you're not implementing the strategy that you intend if you don't spend your time, your money, and your talent in a way that is consistent with your intentions. In your life, there are going to be constant demands for your time and attention. How are you going to decide which of those demands gets resources? The trap many people fall into is to allocate their time to whoever screams loudest, and their talent to whatever offers them the fastest reward. That's a dangerous way to build a strategy.

All of these factors—priorities, balancing plans with opportunities, and allocating your resources—combine to create your strategy. The process is continuous: even as your strategy begins to take shape, you'll learn new things, and new problems and opportunities will always emerge. They'll feed back in; the cycle is continuous.

If you can understand and manage this strategy process, you'll have the best shot at getting it right—of having a career that you will truly love.

Even if you don't end up getting to be an astronaut.

# CHAPTER TWO

# *What Makes Us Tick*

*It's impossible to have a meaningful conversation about happiness without understanding what makes each of us tick. When we find ourselves stuck in unhappy careers—and even unhappy lives—it is often the result of a fundamental misunderstanding of what really motivates us.*

~

## The Importance of Getting Motivation Right

When I was running CPS Technologies, a company that I founded with several MIT professors early in my career, I had an epiphany of sorts about what motivates us. One summer Saturday, we had a company picnic for our employees' families in a park near our laboratories. There was nothing fancy about it, but it was a welcome opportunity to get a three-dimensional perspective of our colleagues' lives.

I walked to the periphery of the group after everyone had arrived, just to figure out who belonged to whom. Out of the corner of my eye, I saw Diana, one of our scientists, and her husband, playing with their two children. Diana had a key position in the lab: she was an analytical chemist. Her job was to help the other scientists use our company's specialized equipment so that they could know what elements were present in the compounds they created or with which they were working. By definition, waiting until the results came back from the tests Diana ran occasionally frustrated some of the twenty or so scientists on the team—each of whom needed his or her test run as the highest priority. But it frustrated Diana even more. She wanted to help everyone, but as a start-up we couldn't buy unlimited equipment. So there were a limited number of machines and only ten hours in Diana's workday. As a result, her days were often filled with turf battles.

But that's not what I saw at that moment. Instead, I was impressed by the love Diana and her husband clearly shared with their two children. Seeing her there, I began to gain a perspective of Diana in the full context of her life. She wasn't just a scientist. She was a mother and a wife, whose mood, whose happiness, and whose sense of self-worth had a huge impact on her family. I began to think about what it must be like in her house in the morning, as she said good-bye to her family on her way to work.

Then I saw Diana in my mind's eye as she came home to her family ten hours later, on a day that had gone badly. She felt underappreciated, frustrated, and demeaned; she learned little that was new. In that moment I felt like I saw how her day at work negatively affected the way she interacted in the evening with her husband and their young children.

This vision in my mind then fast-forwarded to the end of another day. On the one hand, she was so engaged by the experiment she was doing that she wanted to stay at work; but on the other, she was so looking forward to spending time with her husband and children that she clearly wanted to be at home. On that day, I saw her driving home with greater self-esteem—feeling that she had learned a lot, having been recognized in a positive way for achieving valuable things, and played a significant role in the success of some important initiatives for several scientists and for the company. I felt like I could see her go into her home at the end of that day with a replenished reservoir of esteem that profoundly affected her interaction with her husband and those two lovely children. And I also knew how she'd feel going into work the next day—motivated and energized.

It was a profound lesson.

## Do Incentives Make the World Go Round?

Six years later, as a new professor, I was standing at the front of a Harvard classroom teaching Technology and Operations Management, a required first-year course for all of our MBA students. In the discussion that day about the case study on a big materials company, a student recommended a way to resolve a conflict with one of their most critical customers.

She suggested the company assign a key engineer, Bruce Stevens, to this project—in addition to his other responsibilities. I questioned her: "Asking Bruce to do this makes sense in isolation. But getting Bruce to actually make this his highest priority, on top of an overflowing plate of other responsibilities—isn't that going to be hard?"

"Just give him an incentive," was her reply.

"Wow—that sure is a simple answer. What kind of incentive do you have in mind?" I asked.

"Just give him a bonus if he gets it done on time," she responded.

"The problem," I said, "is that he has other responsibilities on other projects as well. If he focuses on this as his top priority, he's going to fall behind on those other projects. So then what are you going to do—give him another financial incentive to motivate him to work harder on all the other projects?" I pointed to a statement in the case about Bruce. He was clearly a driven man, who routinely worked seventy-hour weeks.

When the student said that's exactly what she would do, I pushed her harder. "All the other employees will see that you are giving Bruce a bonus. Aren't they going to demand that you treat them similarly? And where does this all lead? Do you feel like paying them specifically for every assignment— moving to a piecemeal system?" I pointed out that in the case the typical engineers in this company were working very hard every day without incentives. "They seem to love their work, don't they?" I asked.

Another student then added, "I don't think you can pay Bruce an incentive—it's against the policy of the company.

Pay-for-performance bonuses are typically only given to general managers in business units, not to engineers, because it is at the managerial level where revenues and costs come together. Below that, employees have responsibility only for a piece of the puzzle, so incentives can throw things out of balance."

"Oh," I said. "Let me understand what you're saying. In this company, a lot of the senior executives used to be engineers. During that period of their lives, they seemed to be motivated by the work itself. They didn't need incentives—right? So then what happened? When they became executives, did they morph into other beings—types of people that needed financial incentives to work hard? Is that what you are telling me?"

As the discussion in the class continued that day, I sensed a broadening rift between my world and that of some of my students. In their world, it seemed that incentives made the world go round. And in mine—well, I had worked with Diana and her colleagues.

How could we see something so fundamental in such different ways?

## A Better Theory of Motivation

The answer lies in a deep chasm about how the concepts of incentives and motivation relate to each other. There are two broad camps on this question.

Back in 1976, two economists, Michael Jensen and William Meckling, published a paper that has been committed to memory by those in the first camp. The paper, which has been one of the most widely cited of the past three decades, focused on a problem known as agency theory, or *incentive theory*: why don't managers always behave in a way that is in the best interest of shareholders? The root cause, as Jensen and Meckling saw it, is that people work in accordance with how you pay them. The takeaway was that you have to align the interests of executives with the interests of shareholders. That way, if the stock goes up, executives are compensated better, and it makes both shareholders and executives happy. Although Jensen and Meckling didn't specifically argue for huge pay packages, their thinking about what causes executives to focus on some things and not others is financial incentives. Indeed, the drive toward top performance has been widely used as an argument for skyrocketing compensation under the guise of "aligning incentives."

It is not just my students who have become believers in this theory. Many managers have adopted Jensen and Meckling's underlying thinking—believing that when you need to convince others that they should do one thing and not another, you just need to pay them to do what you want them to do, when you want them to do it. It's easy, it's measurable; in essence, you are able to simply delegate management to a formula. Even parents can default to thinking that external rewards are the most effective way to motivate the behavior they want from their children—for example, offering their children a financial reward as an incentive for every A on a report card.

One of the best ways to probe whether you can trust the advice that a theory is offering you is to look for anomalies—

something that the theory cannot explain. Remember our story about birds, feathers, and flight? The early aviators might have seen some warning signs in their rudimentary analysis of flight had they examined what their beliefs or theories could not explain. Ostriches have wings and feathers but can't fly. Bats have wings but no feathers, and they are great fliers. And flying squirrels have neither wings nor feathers . . . and they get by.

The problem with principal-agent, or incentives, theory is that there are powerful anomalies that it cannot explain. For example, some of the hardest-working people on the planet are employed in nonprofits and charitable organizations. Some work in the most difficult conditions imaginable— disaster recovery zones, countries gripped by famine and flood. They earn a fraction of what they would if they were in the private sector. Yet it's rare to hear of managers of non-profits complaining about getting their staff motivated.

You might dismiss these workers as idealists. But the military attracts remarkable people, too. They commit their lives to serving their country. But they are not doing it for financial compensation. In fact, it's almost the opposite— working in the military is far from the best-paid job you can take. Yet in many countries, including the United States, the military is considered a highly effective organization. And a lot of people who work in the military get a deep sense of satisfaction from their work.

How, then, do we explain what is motivating them if it's not money?

Well, there is a second school of thought—often called

*two-factor theory,* or *motivation theory*—that turns the incentive theory on its head. It acknowledges that you can pay people to want what you want—over and over again. But *incentives* are not the same as *motivation.* True motivation is getting people to do something because *they want* to do it. This type of motivation continues, in good times and in bad.

Frederick Herzberg, probably one of the most incisive writers on the topic of motivation theory, published a breakthrough article in the *Harvard Business Review,* focusing on exactly this. He was writing for a business audience, but what he discovered about motivation applies equally to us all.

Herzberg notes the common assumption that job satisfaction is one big continuous spectrum—starting with very happy on one end and reaching all the way down to absolutely miserable on the other—is not actually the way the mind works. Instead, satisfaction and dissatisfaction are separate, independent measures. This means, for example, that it's possible to love your job and hate it at the same time.

Let me explain. This theory distinguishes between two different types of factors: hygiene factors and motivation factors.

On one side of the equation, there are the elements of work that, if not done right, will cause us to be dissatisfied. These are called *hygiene factors.* Hygiene factors are things like status, compensation, job security, work conditions, company policies, and supervisory practices. It matters, for example, that you don't have a manager who manipulates you for his own purposes—or who doesn't hold you accountable for things over which you don't have responsibility. Bad hygiene causes dissatisfaction. You have to address and fix bad hygiene to ensure that you are not dissatisfied in your work.

Interestingly, Herzberg asserts that *compensation is a hygiene factor*, not a motivator. As Owen Robbins, a successful CFO and the board member who chaired our compensation committee at CPS Technologies, once counseled me, "Compensation is a death trap. The most you can hope for (as CEO) is to be able to post a list of every employee's name and salary on the bulletin board, and hear every employee say, 'I sure wish I were paid more, but darn it, this list is fair.' Clayton, you might feel like it is easy to manage this company by giving incentives or rewards to people. But if anyone believes that he is working harder but is being paid less than another person, it would be like transplanting cancer into this company." Compensation is a hygiene factor. You need to get it right. But all you can aspire to is that employees will not be mad at each other and the company because of compensation.

This is an important insight from Herzberg's research: if you instantly improve the hygiene factors of your job, you're not going to suddenly love it. At best, you just won't *hate* it anymore. The opposite of *job dissatisfaction* isn't *job satisfaction*, but rather an *absence of job dissatisfaction*. They're not the same thing at all. It *is* important to address hygiene factors such as a safe and comfortable working environment, relationship with managers and colleagues, enough money to look after your family—if you don't have these things, you'll experience dissatisfaction with your work. But these alone won't do anything to make you love your job—they will just stop you from hating it.

## The Balance of Motivators and Hygiene Factors

So, what are the things that will truly, deeply satisfy us, the factors that will cause us to love our jobs? These are what Herzberg's research calls *motivators*. Motivation factors include challenging work, recognition, responsibility, and personal growth. Feelings that you are making a meaningful contribution to work arise from *intrinsic* conditions of the work itself. Motivation is much less about external prodding or stimulation, and much more about what's inside of you, and inside of your work.

Hopefully, you've had experiences in your life that have satisfied Herzberg's motivators. If you have, you'll recognize the difference between that and an experience that merely provides hygiene factors. It might have been a job that emphasized doing work that was truly meaningful to you, that was interesting and challenging, that allowed you to grow professionally, or that provided opportunities to increase your responsibility. Those are the factors that will motivate you—to cause you to love what you're doing. It's what I hope my students hold out for, because I know it can make the difference between dreading or being excited to go to work every day.

The lens of Herzberg's theory gave me real insight into the choices that some of my classmates made in their careers after we graduated. While many of them did find themselves in careers that were highly motivating, my sense was that an unsettling number did not. How is it that people who seem to have the world at their feet end up making deliberate choices that leave them feeling unfulfilled?

Herzberg's work sheds some light on this. Many of my peers had chosen careers using hygiene factors as the primary criteria; income was often the most important of these. On the surface, they had lots of good reasons to do exactly that. Many people view their education as an investment. You give up good years of your working life, years you would otherwise be making a salary. Compounding that is often the need to take out big loans to finance your time at school, sometimes while supporting young families—as I did. You know exactly how much debt you'll have the minute you graduate.

Yet it was not lost on me that many of my classmates had initially come to school for very different reasons. They'd written their entrance essays on their hopes for using their education to tackle some of the world's most vexing social problems or their dreams of becoming entrepreneurs and creating their own businesses.

Periodically, as we were all considering our postgraduation plans, we'd try to keep ourselves honest, challenging each other: "What about doing something important, or something you really love? Isn't that why you came here?" "Don't worry," came back the answer. "This is just for a couple of years. I'll pay off my loans, get myself in a good financial position, then I'll go chase my real dreams."

It was not an unreasonable argument. The pressures we all face—providing for our families, meeting our own expectations and those of our parents and friends, and, for some of us, keeping up with our neighbors—are tough. In the case of my classmates (and many graduating classes since), this manifested itself in taking jobs as bankers, fund managers, consultants, and plenty of other well-regarded positions. For some people, it was a choice of passion—they genuinely loved what they did and those jobs worked out well for them. But for others, it was a choice based on getting a good financial return on their expensive degree.

By taking these jobs, they managed to pay back their student loans. Then they got their mortgages under control and their families in comfortable financial positions. But somehow that early pledge to return to their real passion after a couple of years kept getting deferred. "Just one more year . . ." or "I'm not sure what else I would do now." All the while, their incomes continued to swell.

It wasn't too long, however, before some of them privately admitted that they had actually begun to resent the jobs they'd taken—for what they now realized were the wrong reasons. Worse still, they found themselves stuck. They'd managed to expand their lifestyle to fit the salaries they were bringing in, and it was really difficult to wind that back. They'd made choices early on because of the hygiene factors, not true motivators, and they couldn't find their way out of that trap.

The point isn't that money is the root cause of professional unhappiness. It's not. The problems start occurring when it becomes the priority over all else, when hygiene factors are satisfied but the quest remains only to make more money. Even those engaged in careers that seem to specifi- cally focus on money, like salespeople and traders, are subject to these rules of motivation—it's just that in these profes- sions, money acts as a highly accurate yardstick of success. Traders, for example, feel success and are motivated by be- ing able to predict what is going to happen in the world and then making bets based on those predictions. Being right is almost directly correlated with making money; it is the con- firmation that they are doing their jobs well, the measure they use to compete on. Similarly, salespeople feel success by being able to convince customers that the product or service they're selling will help those customers in their lives. Again, money directly correlates with success—a sale. It's an indica- tor for how well they're doing their jobs. It's not that some of us are fundamentally different beasts—we might find dif- ferent things meaningful or enjoyable—but the theory still works the same way for everyone. If you get motivators at work, Herzberg's theory suggests, you're going to love your job—even if you're not making piles of money. You're going to be motivated.

## Motivation Matters in Places You Might Not Expect

When you really understand what motivates people, it be- comes illuminating in all kinds of situations—not just in people's careers. My two oldest children taught me an impor- tant dimension of Herzberg's theory on motivation. When we bought our first house, I saw a place in the backyard that would be perfect for building a kids' playhouse. Matthew and

Ann were the perfect ages for this kind of activity, and we threw our hearts into this project. We spent weeks selecting the lumber, picking the shingles for the house, working our way up through the platform, the sides, the roof. I'd get the nails most of the way in and let them deliver the finishing blows. It took longer that way, of course, figuring out whose turn it was for every stroke of the hammer and cut of the saw. It was fun, however, to see their feelings of pride. When their friends came to play, the first thing my children would do was take them into the backyard and show them the progress. And when I came home, their first question was when could we get back to work.

But after it was finished, I rarely saw the children in it. The truth was that *having* the house wasn't what really motivated them. It was the *building* of it, and how they felt about their own contribution, that they found satisfying. I had thought the destination was what was important, but it turned out it was the journey.

It is hard to overestimate the power of these motivators— the feelings of accomplishment and of learning, of being a key player on a team that is achieving something meaningful. I shudder to think that I almost bought a kit from which I could have quickly assembled the playhouse myself.

### If You Find a Job You Love . . .

The theory of motivation—along with its description of the roles that incentives and hygiene factors will play—has given me better understanding of how people become successful and happy in their careers. I used to think that if you cared for other people, you need to study sociology or something like it. But when I compared what I imagined was happening in Diana's home after the different days in our labs, I concluded, if you want to help other people, *be a manager.* If done well, management is among the most noble of professions. You are in a position where you have eight or ten hours every day from every person who works for you. You have the opportunity to frame each person's work so that, at the end of every day, your employees will go home feeling like Diana felt on her good day: living a life filled with motivators. I realized that if the theory of motivation applies to me, then I need to be sure that those who work for me have the motivators, too.

The second realization I had is that the pursuit of money can, at best, mitigate the frustrations in your career—yet the siren song of riches has confused and confounded some of the best in our society. In order to really find happiness, you need to continue looking for opportunities that you believe are meaningful, in which you will be able to learn new things, to succeed, and be given more and more responsibility to shoulder. There's an old saying: find a job that you love and you'll never work a day in your life. People who truly love what they do and who think their work is meaningful have a distinct advantage when they arrive at work every day. They throw their best effort into their jobs, and it makes them very good at what they do.

This, in turn, can mean they get paid well; careers that are filled with motivators are often correlated with financial rewards. But sometimes the reverse is true, too—financial rewards can be present without the motivators. In my assessment, it is frightfully easy for us to lose our sense of the difference between what brings money and what causes happiness. You must be careful not to confuse correlation with causality in assessing the happiness we can find in different jobs.

Thankfully, however, these motivators are stable across professions and over time—giving us a sense of "true north" against which we can recalibrate the trajectories of our careers. We should always remember that beyond a certain point, hygiene factors such as money, status, compensation, and job security are much more a by-product of being happy with a job rather than the cause of it. Realizing this frees us to focus on the things that really matter.

~

*For many of us, one of the easiest mistakes to make is to focus on trying to over-satisfy the tangible trappings of professional success in the mistaken belief that those things will make us happy. Better salaries. A more prestigious title. A nicer office. They are, after all, what our friends and family see as signs that we have "made it" professionally. But as soon as you find yourself focusing on the tangible aspects of your job, you are at risk of becoming like some of my classmates, chasing a mirage. The next pay raise, you think, will be the one that finally makes you happy. It's a hopeless quest.*

*The theory of motivation suggests you need to ask yourself a different set of questions than most of us are used to asking.*

*Is this work meaningful to me? Is this job going to give me a chance to develop? Am I going to learn new things? Will I have an opportunity for recognition and achievement? Am I going to be given responsibility? These are the things that will truly motivate you. Once you get this right, the more measurable aspects of your job will fade in importance.*

# CHAPTER THREE

# The Balance of Calculation and Serendipity

*Understanding what makes us tick is a critical step on the path to fulfillment. But that's only half the battle. You actually have to find a career that both motivates you and satisfies the hygiene factors. If it were that easy, however, wouldn't each of us already have done that? Rarely is it so simple. You have to balance the pursuit of aspirations and goals with taking advantage of unanticipated opportunities. Managing this part of the strategy process is often the difference between success and failure for companies; it's true for our careers, too.*

~

## Honda Takes America . . . by Accident

Back in the 1960s, Honda's management decided to try to gain a toehold in the U.S. motorcycle market, which had historically been dominated by a small number of powerhouse motorcycle brands such as Harley-Davidson and some European imports, like Triumph. They strategized that by making motorcycles comparable to those made by these competitors, and selling them at significantly lower prices (at the time, Japanese labor was *very* inexpensive), they ought to be able to steal away 10 percent of the motorcycle import market from the Europeans.

Doing so almost killed Honda. In the first few years, it sold very few bikes—compared to a Harley, a Honda seemed like a poor man's motorcycle. Worse, Honda discovered that its bikes leaked oil when subjected to the long drives at high speeds that were typical in America. This was a real problem; Honda's dealers in America did not have the capability to repair such complicated problems and Honda had to spend what precious few resources it had in America to air-freight these faulty motorcycles back to Japan to fix them. In spite of the problems, Honda persisted with its original strategy—even as it was draining the U.S. division of virtually all its cash.

In addition to the large bikes it sold, Honda had initially shipped a few of its smaller motorcycles to Los Angeles; but no one really expected American customers to buy them. Known as the Super Cub, these bikes were used in Japan primarily for urban deliveries to shops along narrow roads that were crowded with people, cars, and bicycles. They were very different from the big motorcycles American enthusiasts valued. As Honda's resources in Los Angeles got tighter and tighter, it began to allow its employees to use the Super Cubs to run errands around the city.

One Saturday, a member of Honda's team took his Super Cub into the hills west of Los Angeles to ride up and down through the dirt. He really enjoyed it. In the twists and turns of those hills, he could work out the frustrations that had driven him to the hills in the first place—the failing big-bike strategy.

The next weekend, he invited his colleagues to join him. Seeing the Honda guys having so much fun, other people in the hills that day asked where they, too, could buy one of those "dirt bikes." Though they were told that they were not available in America, one by one, they convinced the Honda team to order them from Japan.

Soon after, a buyer for Sears spotted a Honda employee riding around on a little Super Cub and asked whether Sears might sell it through its catalog. Honda's team was cold to the idea, because it would divert them away from their strategy to sell the larger bikes—a strategy that was still not working. Little by little, however, they realized that selling the smaller bikes was keeping Honda's venture in America alive.

No one had imagined that was how Honda's entry in the U.S. market would play out. They had only planned to compete with the likes of Harley. But it was clear that a better opportunity had emerged. Ultimately, Honda's management team recognized what had happened, and concluded that Honda should embrace small bikes as their official strategy. Priced at a quarter of the cost of a big Harley, the Super Cubs were sold not to classic-motorcycle customers, but to an entirely new group of users that came to be called "off-road bikers."

The rest, as they say, is history. The chance idea of one employee releasing his frustration in the hills that day created a new pastime for millions of Americans who didn't fit the profile of a traditional touring-bike owner. It led to Honda's wildly successful strategy of selling the smaller motorcycles through power equipment and sporting-goods stores, instead of traditional motorbike dealers.

Honda's experience in building a new motorcycle business in America highlights the process by which every strategy is formulated and subsequently evolves. As Professor Henry Mintzberg taught, options for your strategy spring from two very different sources. The first source is anticipated opportunities—the opportunities that you can see and choose to pursue. In Honda's case, it was the big-bike market in the United States. When you put in place a plan focused on these anticipated opportunities, you are pursuing a *deliberate* strategy. The second source of options is unanticipated—usually a cocktail of problems and opportunities that emerges while you are trying to implement the deliberate plan or strategy that you have decided upon. At Honda, what was unanticipated were the problems with the big bikes, the costs associated with fixing them, and the opportunity to sell the little Super Cub motorbikes.

The unanticipated problems and opportunities then essentially fight the deliberate strategy for the attention, capital, and hearts of the management and employees. The company has to decide whether to stick with the original plan, modify it, or even replace it altogether with one of the alternatives that arises. The decision sometimes is an explicit decision;

often, however, a modified strategy coalesces from myriad day-to-day decisions to pursue unanticipated opportunities and resolve unanticipated problems. When strategy forms in this way, it is known as *emergent* strategy. The managers of Honda's beachhead in Los Angeles, for example, did not make an explicit decision to completely change strategy, to focus on the low-cost Super Cubs, in an all-day strategy meeting. Rather, they slowly realized that if they stopped selling the big bikes, it would stem the cash-bleed needed to cover the cost of the leaky-oil repairs. And, one by one, as employees ordered more Super Cub bikes from Japan, the path for profitable growth became clear.

When the company's leaders made a clear decision to pursue the new direction, the *emergent* strategy became the new *deliberate* strategy.

But it doesn't stop there. The process of strategy then re-iterates through these steps over and over again, constantly evolving. In other words, strategy is not a discrete analytical event—something decided, say, in a meeting of top managers based on the best numbers and analysis available at the time. Rather, it is a continuous, diverse, and unruly process. Managing it is very hard—the deliberate strategy and the new emerging opportunities fight for resources. On the one hand, if you have a strategy that really is working, you need to deliberately focus to keep everyone working together in the right direction. At the same time, however, that focus can easily cause you to dismiss as a distraction what could actually turn out to be the next big thing.

It may be challenging and unruly, but this is the process by which almost all companies have developed a winning strategy. Walmart is another great example. Many people think of Sam Walton, Walmart's legendary founder, as a visionary. They assume he started his company with a plan to change the world of retailing. But that's not what really happened.

Walton originally intended to build his second store in Memphis, thinking that a larger city could support a larger store. But he ended up opting for the much smaller town of Bentonville, Arkansas, instead—for two reasons. Legend has it, his wife said in no uncertain terms that she would not move to Memphis. He also recognized that having his second store near his first would allow him to share shipments and deliveries more easily, and take advantage of other logistical efficiencies. That, ultimately, taught Walton the brilliant strategy of opening his large stores only in small towns—thereby preempting competition from other discount retailers.

This wasn't how he imagined his business in the beginning. His strategy emerged.

## Balancing Emergent and Deliberate

I'm always struck by how many of my students and the other young people I've worked with think they're supposed to have their careers planned out, step by step, for the next five years. High-achievers, and aspiring high-achievers, too often put pressure on themselves to do exactly this. Starting as early as high school, they think that to be successful they need to have a concrete vision of exactly what it is they want to do with their lives. Underlying this belief is the implicit assumption that they should risk deviating from their vision only if things go horribly wrong.

But having such a focused plan really *only makes sense in certain circumstances.*

In our lives and in our careers, whether we are aware of it or not, we are constantly navigating a path by deciding between our deliberate strategies and the unanticipated alternatives that emerge. Each approach is vying for our minds and our hearts, making its best case to become our actual strategy. Neither is inherently better or worse; rather, which you should choose depends on where you are on the journey. Understanding this—that strategy is made up of these two disparate elements, and that your circumstances dictate which approach is best—will better enable you to sort through the choices that your career will constantly present.

If you have found an outlet in your career that provides both the requisite hygiene factors and motivators, then a deliberate approach makes sense. Your aspirations should be clear, and you know from your present experience that they are worth striving for. Rather than worrying about adjusting to unexpected opportunities, your frame of mind should be focused on how best to achieve the goals you have deliberately set.

But if you haven't reached the point of finding a career that does this for you, then, like a new company finding its way, you need to be emergent. This is another way of saying that if you are in these circumstances, experiment in life. As you learn from each experience, adjust. Then iterate quickly. Keep going through this process until your strategy begins to click.

As you go through your career, you will begin to find the areas of work you love and in which you will shine; you will, hopefully, find a field where you can maximize the motivators and satisfy the hygiene factors. But it's rarely a case of sitting in an ivory tower and thinking through the problem until the answer pops into your head. Strategy almost always emerges from a combination of deliberate and unanticipated opportunities. What's important is to get out there and try stuff until you learn where your talents, interests, and priorities begin to pay off. When you find out what really works for you, then it's time to flip from an emergent strategy to a deliberate one.

## When the *Wall Street Journal* Didn't Respond

I might not have had the right language to describe it at the time, but navigating between deliberate and emergent opportunities is essentially how I ended up being a professor, a job that I love. It took me years to get it right.

In fact, I've had three careers: first as a consultant, then as an entrepreneur and manager, and now as an academic—none of which I planned. When I was a freshman in college, I decided that I wanted to become the editor of the *Wall Street Journal*, a newspaper I deeply admired. This was my deliberate strategy. One of my professors told me that I was a good writer—but rather than majoring in journalism, I'd have a better chance of distinguishing myself in a field of thousands of job applicants if I knew the field of economics and business. So I studied economics as an undergraduate student at BYU and also at Oxford. Then I pursued my MBA at Harvard.

At the end of my first year in the MBA program, I applied for a summer position at the *Wall Street Journal*. I never got a reply. I was crushed, but an internship at a consulting firm emerged. It wasn't the *Wall Street Journal*, but I knew that I could learn a lot by helping clients solve really interesting problems, and I hoped that would make me even more attractive to the *Journal*. Another consulting firm then offered to pay the full cost of my second MBA year if I would take a postgraduation job with them. We were so broke that I decided to accept it—thinking that I could keep learning about business, and then break loose to start my career with the *Journal*. This was my *emergent* strategy.

Unfortunately for my deliberate plan to be the *Journal*'s editor, I loved the consulting work I was doing. But after five years there, just as Christine and I were deciding it was time to start my real career as a journalist, a friend of mine knocked on my door and asked me to start a company with him. The prospect of starting my own business, facing the challenges myself I'd spent the last few years solving with my clients, really excited me. I just jumped at the chance. Besides, if I could tell the editors of the *Journal* that I had actually founded and run a company, I might be an even better pick for the path to editorship.

We took our company public in mid-1987, shortly before Black Monday. On one hand, we were lucky: we managed to raise capital before the stock market crashed. But from a different point of view, our timing was terrible. Our shares dropped from $10 to $2 in a single day. Our market capitalization became so low that no big institutions would put money into our company. We had planned on being able to raise another round of investment to fund our plan for growth. But without that funding, we became vulnerable. One of our initial investors sold his shares to another venture capitalist, and this sale gave the second venture capitalist enough shares to be in charge of our future. He wanted his own CEO in the top job—and I was fired.

I didn't know it at the time, but this triggered stage three of my emergent strategy.

Several months before I got fired, I had talked with a couple of senior professors at Harvard Business School about another possibility that had been in the back of my mind: whether being a professor was something that I'd be good at. Both had said that I might. So I stood at a fork in the road. Was this the time when I should finally pursue my original deliberate strategy of becoming editor of the *Wall Street Journal*? Or should I try academia? I talked to an additional couple of professors about this, and on the Sunday evening of the very week I had lost my job, one of them called and asked if I would come in the next day. He announced that although the academic year had already started, they had gone out on a limb for me and made the highly unusual decision to admit me to their PhD program then and there. Less than a week after I had been fired, at age thirty-seven, I was a student once more. Emergent strategy again preempted my deliberate path.

Sometime after I finished my doctorate and started my job as a professor, I faced head-on the need to get tenure. At that point, I thought through the fact that although academia had come into my life through an emergent door, in my heart and mind I needed to make this new path my deliberate strategy. To succeed in this arena, I realized I needed to truly focus on it. So that's what I did.

Now, at age fifty-nine and after a twenty-year career in academia, I still wonder occasionally whether it is finally time to try to become editor of the *Wall Street Journal*. Academia became my deliberate strategy—and will stay that way as long as I continue to enjoy what I'm doing. But I have not twisted shut the flow of emergent problems or opportunities. Just as I never imagined thirty years ago I'd end up here, who knows what might be just around the corner?

## What Has to Prove True for This to Work?

Of course, it's easy to say be open to opportunities as they emerge. It's much harder to know which strategy you should actually pursue. Is the current deliberate strategy the best course to continue on, or is it time to adopt a different strategy that is emerging? What happens if ten opportunities present at once? Or if one of them requires a substantial investment on your part just to find out whether it's something that you're going to enjoy? Ideally, you don't want to have to go through medical school to figure out you don't want to be a doctor. So what can you do to figure out what has the best chance of working out for you?

There's a tool that can help you test whether your deliberate strategy or a new emergent one will be a fruitful approach. It forces you to articulate what assumptions need to be proved true in order for the strategy to succeed. The academics who created this process, Ian MacMillan and Rita McGrath, called it "discovery-driven planning," but it might be easier to think about it as "What has to prove true for this to work?"

As simple as it sounds, companies seldom think about whether to pursue new opportunities by asking this question. Instead, they often unintentionally stack the deck for failure from the beginning. They make decisions to go ahead with an investment based on what initial projections suggest will happen, but then they never actually test whether those initial projections are accurate. So, they can find themselves far down the line, adjusting projections and assumptions to fit what is actually happening, rather than making and testing thoughtful choices before they get too far in.

Here's how the flawed process usually works.

An employee or a group of employees come up with an innovative idea for a new product or service; they're enthusiastic about their idea, and they want their colleagues to be, too. But to convince senior management of the idea's potential, they need to come up with a business plan. They are acutely aware that for management to approve the project, the numbers had better look good—but the team often won't *really* know how customers will respond to the idea, what the true costs will turn out to be, and so on. So they guess—they make assumptions. Frequently, planners are sent back to the drawing board to change their guesses. But this is rarely because they have learned new information; instead, innovators and middle managers typically know how good the numbers have to look in order for their proposal to get funded, so they often need to cycle back and "improve" their guesses in order for the proposal to get the go-ahead.

If they do a good enough job convincing management that they're right, they get the green light to proceed with their project. It's only then, once the team begins, that they learn which of those assumptions baked into the financial plan turned out to be right and which were flawed.

See the problem? By the time they have learned which assumptions were right and which were wrong, it's too late to do anything about it. In almost every case of a project failing, mistakes were made in one or more of the critical assumptions upon which the projections and decisions were based. But the company didn't realize that until it was too far down the line in acting on those ideas and plans. Money, time, and energy had already been assigned to the project; the company is 100 percent committed; and the team is now on the line to make it work. Nobody wants to go back to management and say, "You know those assumptions we made? Turns out they weren't so accurate after all . . ." Projects end up getting approved on the basis of incorrect guesses, as opposed to which project is actually most likely to work out.

For example, Disney had launched thriving theme parks in Southern California, Florida, and Tokyo. But their fourth site, outside of Paris, was a disaster for a long time. They lost roughly a billion dollars in the first two years. How could the company get it so wrong on the heels of three enormous successes?

It turns out the initial planning for the Paris site relied on assumptions about the total number of likely visitors and how long they would each stay. The projections were based on population density in concentric circles around the planned park, weather patterns, income levels, and other factors; the plan projected 11 million visitors per year. In the other theme parks, the average Disney guest stayed for three days. So the model multiplied 11 million people by three days, projecting 33 million "guest days" every year. Disney built hotels and infrastructure to support that number.

Well, it turned out that Disney did have around 11 million visitors in that first year. But, on average, they stayed only one day versus the three days they stayed in the other parks.

What happened?

In the other parks, Disney had built forty-five rides. This kept people happily occupied for three days. But Disneyland Paris opened its doors with only fifteen rides. You could do everything in just one day.

Some person way down in the organization made an unconscious assumption about Disneyland Paris being the same size as all the other parks. That assumption then got embedded in the numbers. The folks at the top didn't even know to ask, "What are the most important assumptions that have to prove right for these projections to work—and how will we track them?" If they had, they might have realized very early in the planning that no one knew whether people would still stay at the park for three days if there were only fifteen rides. Instead, Disney had to scramble to recover from the terrible start.

There is a much better way to figure out what is going to work and what isn't. It involves reordering the typical steps involved in planning a new project.

When a promising new idea emerges, financial projections should, of course, be made. But instead of pretending these are accurate, acknowledge that at this point, they are really rough. Since everybody knows that numbers have to look good for management to green-light any project, you don't go through the charade of implicitly encouraging teams to manipulate the numbers to look as strong as possible.

Instead, ask the project teams to compile a list of all the assumptions that have been made in those initial projections. Then ask them: "Which of these assumptions need to prove true in order for us to realistically expect that these numbers will materialize?" The assumptions on this list should be rank-ordered by importance and uncertainty. At the top of the list should be the assumptions that are most important and least certain, while the bottom of the list should be those that are least important and most certain.

Only after you understand the relative importance of

all the underlying assumptions should you green-light the team—but not in the way that most companies tend to do. Instead, find ways to quickly, and with as little expense as possible, test the validity of the most important assumptions.

Once the company understands whether the initial important assumptions are likely to prove true, it can make a much better decision about whether to invest in this project or not.

The logic of taking this approach is compelling—of course everyone wants to achieve gorgeous numbers, so why go through the pretense of asking managers to keep working on them until they look good? Instead, this approach of "What assumptions must prove true?" offers a simple way to keep strategy from going far off-course. It causes teams to focus on what truly matters to get the numbers to materialize. If we ask the right questions, the answers generally are easy to get.

## Before You Take That Job

This type of planning can help you consider job opportunities, too. We all want to be successful and happy in our careers. But it's all too easy to get too far down a path before you've realized that choices aren't working out as you hoped. This tool can help you avoid doing just that.

Before you take a job, carefully list what things others are going to need to do or to deliver in order for you to successfully achieve what *you* hope to do. Ask yourself: "What are the assumptions that have to prove true in order for me to be able to succeed in this assignment?" List them. Are they within your control?

Equally important, ask yourself what assumptions have to prove true for you to be *happy* in the choice you are contemplating. Are you basing your position on extrinsic or intrinsic motivators? Why do you think this is going to be something you enjoy doing? What evidence do you have? Every time you consider a career move, keep thinking about the most important assumptions that have to prove true, and how you can swiftly and inexpensively test if they are valid. Make sure you are being realistic about the path ahead of you.

## The Importance of Testing Assumptions

I wish I'd had the wherewithal at the time to use this tool to help a student avoid a disappointing first job. When she was being recruited, the folks at the venture capital firm where she ended up working told her that they intended to invest 20 percent of their resources in developing-country growth initiatives. That was what my student had hoped to hear. She had worked for several years with a humanitarian organization in Asia before coming to our school, and after graduation she was looking for even bigger opportunities to create new growth companies in emerging countries. It seemed like a perfect fit, and she accepted their employment offer.

But it turned out, in spite of their promises, the firm didn't have the resolve or the resources to deliver. With each new assignment, my student would hope for a developing-country investment, but one never materialized. She had returned from Asia determined to continue working with developing nations, but her assignments continually focused on the United States. In the end she became embittered toward her employer, feeling that the firm and its leaders had deceptively co-opted her time and talents in the prime of her life. She eventually left and had to start all over again.

How could she have used the lens of "What has to prove true?" in assessing this job? A good place to start would have been to look at the characteristics of other firms that have successfully entered the developing world. For example, firms that have a deep commitment to developing countries typically have capital tied to investment there. They have partners dedicated to the practice. Their investors are attracted to the company in part because of its work in the developing world. Perhaps she could have opted for an internship before committing to a full-time job.

If my student had listed out and found ways to test those assumptions, she would likely have recognized that though the firm might have intended to invest in emerging economies, it was quite unlikely that it would really do so. Similarly, it turned out I was just very lucky when making my own professional choices after my undergraduate studies. I never stopped to scrutinize my own assumptions. This would have been a great tool to help me think through what had to prove true for any opportunity in front of me—be it consulting, entrepreneurship, or academia—to be one that I could both be successful at and also enjoy.

In hindsight, I was able to navigate my own journey through a combination of the push and pull of deliberate strategy and being open to unanticipated opportunities. I hope you can, too. I will never declare my career path polished and perfected—there could be exciting unanticipated opportunities out there for me, even at age fifty-nine. Who knows? Maybe the *Wall Street Journal* will still call one day to offer me that job . . .

~

*Hopefully, you're going to go off into the world with an understanding of what makes us tick. But speaking from my own experience, it can be tough to find the right career to do that for you.*

*What we can learn from how companies develop strategy is that although it is hard to get it right at first, success doesn't rely on this. Instead, it hinges on continuing to experiment until you do find an approach that works. Only a lucky few companies start off with the strategy that ultimately leads to success.*

*Once you understand the concept of emergent and deliberate strategy, you'll know that if you've yet to find something that really works in your career, expecting to have a clear vision of where your life will take you is just wasting time. Even worse, it may actually close your mind to unexpected opportunities. While you are still figuring out your career, you should keep the aperture of your life wide open. Depending on your particular circumstances, you should be prepared to experiment with different opportunities, ready to pivot, and continue to adjust your strategy until you find what it is that both satisfies the hygiene factors and gives you all the motivators. Only then does a delib-erate strategy make sense. When you get it right, you'll know.*

*As difficult as it may seem, you've got to be honest with yourself about this whole process. Change can often be diffi-cult, and it will probably seem easier to just stick with what you are already doing. That thinking can be dangerous. You're only kicking the can down the road, and you risk waking up one day, years later, looking into the mirror, asking yourself: "What am I doing with my life?"*

# CHAPTER FOUR

## *Your Strategy Is Not What You Say It Is*

*You can talk all you want about having a strategy for your life, understanding motivation, and balancing aspirations with un-anticipated opportunities. But ultimately, this means nothing if you do not align those with where you actually expend your time, money, and energy.*

*In other words, how you allocate your resources is where the rubber meets the road.*

*Real strategy—in companies and in our lives—is created through hundreds of everyday decisions about where we spend our resources. As you're living your life from day to day, how do you make sure you're heading in the right direction? Watch where your resources flow. If they're not supporting the strategy you've decided upon, then you're not implementing that strategy at all.*

~

## Getting the Measure of Success Wrong

More than a decade ago, Seattle-based SonoSite was founded to make handheld ultrasound equipment—little machines that had the potential to truly change health care. Prior to these machines, the only thing that most family doctors and nurses could do when performing an exam was to listen and feel for problems beneath the skin. As a result, many problems would elude detection until they were more advanced. For twenty years or so, although technology had existed that enabled specialists to look into a patient's body through cart-based ultrasound, CT scan, or MRI machines, this equipment was big and expensive. SonoSite's handheld ultrasound machines, however, made it affordable and easy for primary care doctors and nurse practitioners to see inside their patients' bodies.

SonoSite had two families of handheld products. Its principal product, dubbed the Titan, was about as big as a laptop computer. The other, branded the iLook, was less than half the size of the Titan—and one-third the price. Both machines had enormous potential.

The iLook was not as sophisticated as the Titan, nor as profitable, but it was much more portable. The company's president and CEO, Kevin Goodwin, knew there was a promising market for it—the iLook had managed to generate a thousand sales leads in the first six weeks after its introduction. It became clear that if SonoSite didn't sell it, someone else was likely to develop the same compact, inexpensive technology and disrupt the sales of the more expensive machines—and SonoSite itself.

Eager to see firsthand how customers were responding to the new, smaller product, Goodwin asked to attend a sales call with one of the company's top salespeople.

What happened taught Goodwin a critical lesson.

The salesman sat down with the customer and proceeded to sell the Titan—the laptop ultrasound. He didn't even pull the iLook handheld out of his bag. After fifteen minutes, Goodwin decided to intervene.

"Tell them about the iLook," Goodwin prompted the salesman. But he was completely ignored. The salesman continued to extol the virtues of the Titan. Goodwin waited a few minutes, then leaned over again. "Take the handheld ultrasound machine out of your bag!" he insisted. Again, the salesman completely ignored him. Goodwin asked one of his best salespeople three times to sell the iLook—in front of the customer. Each time, he was completely dismissed.

What was going on? The CEO of the company couldn't persuade his employee to do as he asked?

The salesman wasn't deliberately trying to defy Goodwin. In fact, he was doing exactly what the company wanted him to do—sell the product that provided the highest return.

Goodwin knew that the handheld innovation had enormous long-term potential for the company—perhaps even more than the successful laptop-size model. The problem was, the salespeople were all on commission, and success for them was defined by the total value of their sales and gross margin dollars. It was much easier for Goodwin's best salesman to sell one of the laptop-size ultrasound machines than it was to sell five of the little products. In other words, Goodwin *thought* that he was giving clear instructions into the salesman's ear. But the compensation system was shouting the opposite instructions into his other ear.

## The Paradox of Resource Allocation

At SonoSite, as in nearly every company, this conflict was not an inadvertent oversight. Rather, it is a pervasive paradox—a problem that I've termed in my research as the *innovator's dilemma*. The company's income statement highlighted all the costs that the company was incurring. It also showed all the revenues that SonoSite needed to generate day in and day out, in order to cover those costs—which, by the way, it had to do if it wanted to improve the quality and cost of health care for millions of people. The salespeople would need to sell five iLook handheld devices to generate the profits that a single Titan laptop would provide. And their own commissions were higher when they sold the more expensive laptop device.

The sorts of problems that Kevin Goodwin and his salespeople were wrestling with are some of the most challenging of all—those where the things that make sense don't make sense. Sometimes these problems emerge between departments within a company. At SonoSite, for example, what made sense from the CEO's perspective did not make sense from the salesman's perspective. What made sense to engineers—pushing the frontier of performance in the next products beyond the best of their current products, making them more sophisticated and capable, regardless of expense—was counter to the logic of the company's strategy, which was to make the iLook even smaller and more affordable.

Often even more perplexing, however, is when these problems arise within the mind of the same person: when the right decision for the long term makes no sense for the short term; when the wrong customer to call on is actually the right customer to call on; and when the most important product to sell makes little sense to sell at all.

The decision that the SonoSite case describes introduces the last component in the strategy process: resource allocation. In the prior chapter, we introduced the idea that we decide between deliberate plans and emergent alternatives. In this chapter, we dive much more deeply into this—because in the strategy process, resource allocation is where the rubber meets the road. The resource allocation process determines which deliberate and emergent initiatives get funded and implemented, and which are denied resources. Everything related to strategy inside a company is only *intent* until it gets to the resource allocation stage. A company's vision, plans, and opportunities—and all of its threats and problems—all want priority, vying against one another to become the actual strategy the company implements.

## When Individuals Cause the Problems

Sometimes, a company such as SonoSite causes well-intended staff to go off in the wrong direction when the measures of success for employees are counter to those that will make the company successful. A company can also be at fault when it prioritizes the short term over the long.

But sometimes individuals themselves are at the root of the problem.

Apple Inc. shows how the differences between individuals' priorities and a company's priorities can prove fatal. Through most of the 1990s, after founder Steve Jobs had been forced out, Apple's ability to deliver the fantastic products it had become renowned for simply stopped. Without Jobs's discipline at the company, daylight began to emerge between Apple's intended strategy and its actual one—and Apple began to flounder.

For example, Apple's attempt to create a next-generation operating system to compete with Microsoft during the mid-nineties—codenamed Copland—slipped numerous times. Though it was a purported priority for the company, Apple just couldn't seem to deliver it. Management kept telling everyone—press, employees, and shareholders—how important it was. But on the front lines, the senior management's sense of what the market wanted made little sense to the troops. Engineers seemed more interested in dreaming up new ideas than finishing what had already been promised for Copland. Without Jobs, individuals were able to get away with spending their time on ideas they were excited about, regardless of whether they matched the company's goals. Eventually, Ellen Hancock, Apple's chief technology officer at the time, scrapped Copland altogether, recommending the company buy something else instead.

When Jobs returned as CEO in 1997, he immediately set to work fixing the underlying resource allocation problem. Rather than allowing everyone to focus on their own sense of priorities, Jobs brought Apple back to its roots: to make the best products in the world, change the way people think about using technology in their lives, and provide a fantastic user experience. Anything not aligned with that got scrapped; people who did not agree were yelled at, abased, or fired. Soon, people began to understand that if they didn't allocate their resources in a way that was consistent with Apple's priorities, they would land in hot water. More than anything else, the deep internal understanding of what Jobs prioritized is why Apple has been able to deliver on what it says it's going to do, and is a big part of why the company has been able to regain its status among the world's most successful.

## The Dangers of Getting the Time Frame Wrong

But individuals are far from the only cause of this problem. In fact, if you study the root causes of business disasters, over and over you'll find a predisposition toward endeavors that offer immediate gratification over endeavors that result in long-term success. Many companies' decision-making systems are designed to steer investments to initiatives that offer the most tangible and immediate returns, so companies often favor these and shortchange investments in initiatives that are crucial to their long-term strategies.

To illustrate how pervasive the innovator's dilemma is between short- and long-term options, let's examine another oft-emulated company, Unilever, one of the world's largest providers of products in foods, personal care, and laundry and cleaning. In order to grow, Unilever has invested billions of dollars to create breakthrough innovations that will produce significant new growth business for the corporation. In baseball terms, however, instead of exciting new "home run" products, its innovators often produce instead bunts and singles—year after year. Why?

After studying their efforts for over a decade, I concluded that the reason is that Unilever (and many corporations like them) inadvertently *teach* their best employees to hit only bunts and singles. Its senior executives every year identify next-generation leaders (high-potential leaders, or "HPLs") from their worldwide operations. To train this cadre so that as senior executives they will be able to move around the globe from one assignment to the next with aplomb, they cycle the HPLs through assignments of eighteen months to two years in every functional group—finance, operations, sales, HR, marketing, and so on—in a sampling of products and markets.

As they finish each assignment, the quality of the work they have completed typically determines the prominence of the next assignment they receive. HPLs who log a series of successful assignments "earn" the best subsequent assignments, and are more likely to become the company's next senior executives.

Think about this from the perspective of the young employees, all of whom were thrilled to be picked for this development program. What projects are they most likely to covet, in each of their assignments? In theory, they should champion products and processes that will be key to Unilever's future success five and ten years ahead. But the results of those efforts, only available many years later, will garnish the record of whoever is in that specific assignment at that time—not the person whose insight initiated it. If, instead, the HPLs focus on delivering results they know can be seen and measured within twenty-four months—even if that method isn't the best approach—they know that the people running the program will be able to assess their contribution to a completed project. As long as they have something to show for their efforts, they know they'll have a shot at an even better next assignment. The system rewards tomorrow's senior executives for being decidedly focused on the short term—inadvertently undermining the company's goals.

Misaligned incentives are pervasive. For example, America is unable to change its Social Security, Medicare, and other entitlement programs—despite the fact that everyone agrees that these programs are driving the country over a precipitous cliff toward bankruptcy. Why? Members of the House of Representatives stand for reelection every two years. These representatives, rightly or wrongly, are convinced that if America is to be saved, they personally need to be reelected in order to lead that effort.

It is broadly known how to solve these problems. But no members of the House will pull these solutions out of their bags, to "sell" them to their customer, the voters. The reason is that there are so many people who benefit from the entitlements that they will vote out of office anyone who pulls the solution out of his or her bag. Despite the fact that senior statesmen (who are retired and no longer need to stand for reelection) are sitting right next to the members and, over and over, urge the current representatives to pull the solutions out of their bags, the elected officials simply cannot do it. Somebody ought to organize a conference in Maui where SonoSite's salespeople, Unilever's HPLs, and members of Congress can commiserate with each other about the tug-of-war between what they're being told are their priorities and what they are actually being encouraged to do.

It's not an easy game to win.

## Allocation Resources Among Your "Businesses"

In the words of Andy Grove: "To understand a company's strategy, look at what they actually do rather than what they say they will do." Resource allocation works pretty much the same way in our lives and careers. Gloria Steinem framed strategy for her world as Andy Grove did for his: "We can tell our values by looking at our checkbook stubs." The dilemma of what machine to pull out of a salesperson's bag is very similar to the dilemma we all face near the end of a workday: do I spend another half hour at work to get something extra done, or do I go home and play with my children?

Here is a way to frame the investments that we make in the strategy that becomes our lives: we have resources— which include personal time, energy, talent, and wealth— and we are using them to try to grow several "businesses" in our personal lives. These include having a rewarding relationship with our spouse or significant other; raising great children; succeeding in our careers; contributing to our church or community; and so on. Unfortunately, however, our resources are limited and these businesses are competing for them. It's exactly the same problem that a corporation has. How should we devote our resources to each of these pursuits?

Unless you manage it mindfully, your personal resource allocation process will decide investments for you according to the "default" criteria that essentially are wired into your brain and your heart. As is true in companies, your resources are not decided and deployed in a single meeting or when you review your calendar for the week ahead. It is a continuous process—and you have, in your brain, a filter for making choices about what to prioritize.

But it's a messy process. People ask for your time and energy every day, and even if you are focused on what's important to you, it's still difficult to know which are the right choices. If you have an extra ounce of energy or a spare thirty minutes, there are a lot of people pushing you to spend them here rather than there. With so many people and projects wanting your time and attention, you can feel like you are not in charge of your own destiny. Sometimes that's good: opportunities that you never anticipated emerge. But other times, those opportunities can take you far off course, as was true for so many of my classmates.

The danger for high-achieving people is that they'll unconsciously allocate their resources to activities that yield the most immediate, tangible accomplishments. This is often in their careers, as this domain of their life provides the most concrete evidence that they are moving forward. They ship a product, finish a design, help a patient, close a sale, teach a class, win a case, publish a paper, get paid, get promoted. They leave college and find it easy to direct their precious energy into building a career. The students in my class are often like this—they leave school with an intense drive to have something to show for their education.

In fact, how you allocate your own resources can make your life turn out to be exactly as you hope or very different from what you intend.

For those of my classmates who inadvertently invested in lives of hollow unhappiness, I can't help but believe that their troubles stemmed from incorrectly allocating resources. To a person, they were well-intended; they wanted to provide for their families and offer their children the best possible opportunities in life. But they somehow spent their resources on paths and byways that dead-ended in places that they had not imagined.

They prioritized things that gave them immediate returns—such as a promotion, a raise, or a bonus—rather than the things that require long-term work, the things that you won't see a return on for decades, like raising good children. And when those immediate returns were delivered, they used them to finance a high-flying lifestyle for themselves and their families: better cars, better houses, and better vacations. The problem is, lifestyle demands can quickly lock in place the personal resource allocation process. "I can't devote less time to my job because I won't get that promotion—and I need that promotion . . ."

Intending to build a satisfying personal life alongside their professional life, making choices specifically to provide a better life for their family, they unwittingly overlook their spouse and children. Investing time and energy in these relationships doesn't offer them that same immediate sense of achievement that a fast-track career does. You can neglect your relationship with your spouse, and on a day-to-day basis, it doesn't seem as if things are deteriorating. Your spouse is still there when you get home every night. And kids find new ways to misbehave all the time. It's really not until twenty years down the road that you can put your hands on your hips and say, "We raised good kids."

In fact, you'll often see the same sobering pattern when looking at the personal lives of many ambitious people. Though they may believe that their family is deeply important to them, they actually allocate fewer and fewer resources to the things they would say matter most.

Few people set out to do this. The decisions that cause it to happen often seem tactical—just small decisions that they think won't have any larger impact. But as they keep allocating resources in this way—and although they often won't realize it—they're implementing a strategy vastly different from what they intend.

~

*A strategy—whether in companies or in life—is created through hundreds of everyday decisions about how you spend your time, energy, and money. With every moment of your time, every de-*

*cision about how you spend your energy and your money, you are making a statement about what really matters to you. You can talk all you want about having a clear purpose and strategy for your life, but ultimately this means nothing if you are not investing the resources you have in a way that is consistent with your strategy. In the end, a strategy is nothing but good intentions unless it's effectively implemented.*

*How do you make sure that you're implementing the strategy you truly want to implement? Watch where your resources flow*—the resource allocation process. *If it is not supporting the strategy you've decided upon, you run the risk of a serious problem. You might think you are a charitable person, but how often do you really give your time or money to a cause or an organization that you care about? If your family matters most to you, when you think about all the choices you've made with your time in a week, does your family seem to come out on top? Because if the decisions you make about where you invest your blood, sweat, and tears are not consistent with the person you aspire to be, you'll never become that person.*

# SECTION II

~

## Finding Happiness in Your Relationships

The happiest moments of my life have been the few which I have passed at home in the bosom of my family.

—*Thomas Jefferson*

So FAR, WE have focused on how to use the strategy process to find fulfillment in your career. I started out by discussing what truly motivates all of us—in effect, the priorities that will lead us to experience happiness in what we do at work. I then showed you how to balance a deliberate plan for finding a career that delivers you those motivations, alongside the unexpected opportunities that will always arise along the way. And finally, we talked about allocating our resources in a manner that is consistent with all these concepts. Get the three parts of the strategy process right, and you'll be on track to a career that you truly love.

Many of us are wired with a high need for achievement, and your career is going to be the most immediate way to pursue that. In our own internal resource allocation process, it will be incredibly tempting to invest every extra hour of time or ounce of energy in whatever activity yields the clearest and most immediate evidence that we've achieved something. Our careers provide such evidence in spades.

But there is much more to life than your career. The person you are at work and the amount of time you spend there will impact the person you are outside of work with your family and close friends. In my experience, high-achievers focus a great deal on becoming the person they want to be at work—and far too little on the person they want to be at home. Investing our time and energy in raising wonderful children or deepening our love with our spouse often doesn't return clear evidence of success for many years. What this leads us to is over-investing in our careers, and under-investing in our families—starving one of the most important parts of our life of the resources it needs to flourish.

It should be becoming clear that the answers to all three of our questions are deeply connected. Try as you might, it's very hard to wall off different parts of your life. Your career priorities—the motivators that will make you happy at work—are simply one part of a broader set of priorities in your life, priorities that include your family, your friends, your faith, your health, and so on. Similarly, the way you balance your plans with unanticipated opportunities, and allocate your resources—your time and energy—does not stop when you walk out the door of your office. You're making decisions about these every moment of your life. You will be constantly pressured, both at home and at work, to give people and projects your attention. How do you decide who gets what? Whoever makes the most noise? Whoever grabs you first? You have to make sure that you allocate your resources in a way that is consistent with your priorities. You have to make sure that your own measures of success are aligned with your most important concern. And you have to make sure that you're thinking about all these in the right time frame—overcome the natural tendency to focus on the short term at the expense of the long term.

It's rarely easy. Even when you know what your true priorities are, you'll have to fight to uphold them in your own mind every day. For example: like many of you, I suspect, I'm naturally drawn to interesting problems and challenges. I can lose myself in one for hours; solving it will give me a short-term "high." It would be easy for me to stay late at work noodling on one of these challenges, or to be stopped in the hallway to have an interesting conversation with a colleague, or to answer the phone and find myself agreeing to work on something completely new and be genuinely excited by the prospect.

But I know that spending my time this way is not consistent with my priorities. I've had to force myself to stay aligned with what matters most to me by setting hard stops, barriers, and boundaries in my life—such as leaving the office at six every day so that there is daylight time to play catch with my son, or to take my daughter to a ballet lesson—to keep myself true to what I most value. If I didn't do this, I know I would be tempted to measure my success that day by having solved a problem rather than getting the time I love with my family. I have to be clear with myself that the long-term payoff of investing my resources in this sphere of my life will be far more profound. Work can bring you a sense of fulfillment—but it pales in comparison to the enduring happiness you can find in the intimate relationships that you cultivate with your family and close friends.

In the following chapters, we're going to explore this more. But there is one topic that deserves some particular context. Whenever it is that you're dealing with other human beings, it's not always possible to control how things turn out; nowhere is this more true than with children. Even if you're armed with an abundance of love and good intentions, it's a complicated world: kids have unprecedented access to ideas from everywhere—their friends, the media, the Internet. The most determined parent will still find that it is almost impossible to control all these influences. On top of that, each child is wired differently. We rarely have children who are exactly like us—or like each other—something that often comes as a surprise to new parents. Our children aren't always interested in the same things that we were, and they don't always behave the way we would have.

As such, there is no one-size-fits-all approach that anyone can offer you. The hot water that softens a carrot will harden an egg. As a parent, you will try many things with your child that simply won't work. When this happens, it can be very easy to view it as a failure. Don't. If anything, it's the opposite. If you recount our discussion of emergent and deliberate strategy—the balance between your plans and unanticipated opportunities—then you'll know that getting something wrong doesn't mean you have failed. Instead, you have just learned what does not work. You now know to try something else.

It also goes without saying that there are some tools available to businesses that we just can't use in our personal lives. For example, organizations have the ability to hire and fire employees to shape the culture they want. You can't hire your kids for cultural fit. You don't get to choose how they're wired. And much as you might want to sometimes, you can't fire them. (Thankfully, they can't fire you, either.)

Nevertheless, what I offer you in the following chapters can help because many of the problems we encounter in the workplace are often fundamentally the same in nature as the problems we encounter at home. If you want to be a good spouse, a good parent, and a good friend, then these next theories will give you a much better chance of creating the kind of family you aspire to and the kind of friendships that last a lifetime. But nothing can promise you perfect results. What I can promise you is that you won't get it right if you don't commit to keep trying.

Intimate, loving, and enduring relationships with our family and close friends will be among the sources of the deepest joy in our lives. They are worth fighting for. In this section, we are going to explore how you can nourish these relationships—and, just as important, avoid damaging them—as you continue upon your life's journey.

# CHAPTER FIVE

## The Ticking Clock

*The relationships you have with family and close friends are going to be the most important sources of happiness in your life. But you have to be careful. When it seems like everything at home is going well, you will be lulled into believing that you can put your investments in these relationships onto the back burner. That would be an enormous mistake. By the time serious problems arise in those relationships, it often is too late to repair them. This means, almost paradoxically, that the time when it is most important to invest in building strong families and close friendships is when it appears, at the surface, as if it's not necessary.*

~

## A Spectacularly Big Failure

Few companies have launched their product with more fan-fare than the Iridium Satellite Network—mobile phones that would allow people to call from literally anywhere on the planet by tapping into a complex celestial network of satellites. Vice President Al Gore helped launch Iridium's product by placing its first call—to Alexander Graham Bell's grandson. Iridium was largely funded and managed by Motorola, one of the most highly regarded microelectronics and telecommunications companies in the world.

Company executives and Wall Street analysts alike confidently projected that Iridium would revolutionize mobile communications, attracting millions of users. The Iridium team had conducted extensive research to assess the market—and it was there. They had defied the odds and managed to convince governments around the world to allocate spectrum to the signals that the satellites needed.

Traditional cell phones connected users to each other by relying on towers to relay signals from one to the next. It wasn't always reliable; if there wasn't a tower in a critical location that could pass the call along, the system dropped the call. The Iridium strategy, in contrast, would send each call from a customer to a satellite—which would then send the call back to earth, to the intended recipient. If the customer was on the other side of the earth, the satellite would send the signal to another satellite that was positioned to send the call to the recipient. That meant that you could call someone from almost anywhere on earth.

And who wouldn't want the ability to call her father in Baltimore when she stands triumphant on top of Mount Everest?

Iridium had access to some world-class expertise and had overcome some seemingly insurmountable hurdles. But there were some fundamental flaws in Iridium's strategy. Simply running through the exercise of "What assumptions need to prove true?" in order for the financial model of Iridium to work would have surfaced these issues. One of these was that customers needed to get comfortable carrying a handset in a briefcase, not a pocket or purse—because it weighed a pound. This was because it needed a big battery, to boost its signal to a satellite, not a local tower. An additional assumption that needed to prove true was that while the signal from the top of Everest to the nearest satellite was likely to be clear, Dad needed to be outside in Baltimore to receive his daughter's call—there could not be a roof creating interference between Dad and the satellite; and so on.

But after $6 billion in investment and less than a year after that first phone call was placed, the company was forced to admit defeat and declare bankruptcy. Iridium didn't emerge from bankruptcy for a decade and investors lost their shirts. After winding its way through Chapter 11, Iridium was sold to a new group of investors for $25 million—a fire-sale price.

Why did the executives of Motorola and its coinvestors fuel so much capital into such a risky venture? The theory that we call "good money and bad money" offers an answer.

## A Theory of Good and Bad Capital

At a basic level, there are two goals investors have when they put money into a company: growth and profitability. Neither is easy. Professor Amar Bhide showed in his *Origin and Evolution of New Business* that 93 percent of all companies that ultimately become successful had to abandon their original strategy—because the original plan proved not to be viable. In other words, successful companies don't succeed because they have the right strategy at the beginning; but rather, because they have money left over after the original strategy fails, so that they can pivot and try another approach. Most of those that fail, in contrast, spend all their money on their original strategy—which is usually wrong.

The theory of good money and bad money essentially frames Bhide's work as a simple assertion. When the winning strategy is not yet clear in the initial stages of a new business, good money from investors needs to be *patient* for growth but *impatient* for profit. It demands that a new company figures out a viable strategy as fast as and with as little investment as possible—so that the entrepreneurs don't spend a lot of money in pursuit of the wrong strategy. Given that 93 percent of companies that ended up being successful had to change their initial strategy, any capital that demands that the early company become very big, very fast, will almost always drive the business off a cliff instead. A big company will burn through money much faster, and a big organization is much harder to change than a small one. Motorola learned this lesson with Iridium.

That is why capital that seeks growth before profits is bad capital.

But the reason why both types of capital appear in the name of the theory is that once a viable strategy has been found, investors need to change what they seek—they should become *impatient* for growth and *patient* for profit. Once a profitable and viable way forward has been discovered—success now depends on scaling out this model.

## Planting Saplings When You Decide You Need Shade

Some of the most frequent offenders in failing to abide by this theory are big investors and successful existing businesses looking to invest in new growth businesses. The way in which this happens is through a predictable and simple three-step process, as articulated by Matthew Olson and Derek van Bever in *Stall Points*.

The first step is that because the probability is so high that the initial plan isn't viable, the investor needs to invest in the next wave of growth even while the original business is strong and growing—to give the new initiative the time to figure out a viable strategy. Despite this, the owner of the capital postpones the investment because today it seems unwarranted, given the strength of the core business and its incessant appetite for more capital investment and executive bandwidth. Deal with tomorrow tomorrow.

In the next step, tomorrow arrives. The original core business has become mature and stops growing. The owner of the capital suddenly realizes that he should have invested several years earlier in the next growth business, so that when the core business stalled, the next engine of growth and profit would already be taking over as the engine for growth and profit. Instead, the engine just isn't there.

Third, the owner of the capital demands that any business that he invests in must become very big, very fast. For a venture that generates $40 million of business, to grow at a 25 percent annual rate you'll need to find $10 million of new growth next year. But if a venture has grown to become a $40 *billion* business and wants to continue growing 25 percent next year, you'll need to find $10 *billion* in new business. The stakes—and pressure—become enormous. To accelerate it faster, shareholders pour lots of capital into these initiatives. But all too often, this abundant capital gives fuel to the entrepreneurs, allowing them to recklessly pursue the wrong strategy aggressively. As these new businesses drive at full speed over the cliff, analysts construct unique stories for why each one failed.

This theory explains how and why Honda ultimately succeeded in its attack against the U.S. motorcycle industry, whereas Motorola failed with Iridium. Ironically, Honda succeeded because the company was so financially constrained in its early days, it was forced to be patient for growth while it figured out its profit model. If Honda had had more resources to give to its U.S. operations, it might have been willing to throw more money into continuing to pursue the large-motorcycle strategy, even though it was unlikely to be profitable. As an investment, that would have been *bad money*. Instead, Honda almost had no choice but to focus on the

Super Cub, because, to survive, it *needed* the money the little bike generated. That was a big part of the reason that Honda ended up doing so well in the United States—its investment was forced to abide by the theory.

The alternative to this approach is to focus on the opposite: invest to see a business grow big quickly and figure out how to be profitable down the line. This is what Motorola did with Iridium. History is littered with failed companies that tried to take this path; it's almost always an ineffective shortcut to success.

Because of the causal mechanism described in the good money and bad money theory, for most companies, there will come a day of reckoning, a day when the company's main business stumbles or stops growing and new sources of revenue are needed, and needed quickly. If a company has ignored investing in new businesses until it *needs* those new sources of revenue and profits, it's already too late. It's like planting saplings when you decide you need more shade. It's just not possible for those trees to grow large enough to create shade overnight. It takes years of patient nurturing to have any chance of the trees growing tall enough to provide it.

**Investing for Future Happiness**

It can be all too easy to default to a bad money approach in our lives, too. Many of us thrive on the intensity of a demanding job—one that we believe in and enjoy. We like proving what we can do under pressure. Our projects, our clients, and our colleagues challenge us. We invest ourselves in our jobs.

But in order to accomplish all this, we start to think of our jobs as requiring all our attention—and that's exactly what we give them.

We call in to work from remote vacation spots. In fact, we may never take all the vacation days we're allowed; there's simply too much to be done. Work becomes how we identify ourselves. We take our smartphones with us everywhere, checking for news constantly—as if not being connected all the time would mean we're going to miss out on something really important. We expect the people who are closest to us to accept that our schedule is simply too demanding to make much time for them. After all, they want to see us succeed, too, right? We find ourselves forgetting to return e-mails and phone calls from our friends and our families; neglecting birthdays and other celebrations that used to be important to us.

Unfortunately, the same consequences that businesses face for failing to invest for the future apply to us, too.

While most of us do have a deliberate strategy of creating deep, love-filled relationships with members of our family and our friends, in reality we invest in a strategy for our lives that we would never have aspired to: having shallow friendships with many but deep friendships with none; becoming divorced, sometimes repeatedly; and having children who feel alienated from us within our own homes, or who are raised by a stepparent sometimes thousands of miles away.

And we can't turn the clock back.

One of my neighbors, whom I'll call Steve, told me years ago that he had always wanted to own and operate his own business. He had many opportunities to work for and learn from someone else in his profession—and at very attractive compensation, too—but he was never willing to part with his dream of being his own boss. That meant long hours at work, learning from relatively simple mistakes to build up his own firm. His friends and family were understanding, though; after all, Steve wasn't doing it just because it was important to him. He was doing it to provide for his family.

The meagerness of Steve's investments of time in his family ultimately took its toll, however. Just as his company was finally taking off, his marriage fell apart. When he needed the support of siblings and friends as he navigated the pain of divorce, he found himself quite alone. He sought the returns on an investment he hadn't made. No one intentionally deserted him in his hour of need; it was just that he had neglected them for so long that they no longer felt close to him and they worried that any intervention might be considered an intrusion.

Steve moved out of his house into a small apartment across town. He tried to make it nice for his two sons and two daughters when they visited. Though he'd always left such things to his wife when they were married, he worked hard to try to come up with new things to do and ways to make their time together fun. But he was fighting an uphill battle. By the time his children were in middle school, the idea of spending every other weekend with Steve during his "visiting privileges" was not that appealing to them. They had to leave their friends and their home to move in with their dad in his spartan apartment—only to go out to dinner, work in the business with him, or maybe to see a movie. It soon lost its charm. Just as Steve was feeling he needed time with his children, they started opting out of their visits with Dad whenever they could.

Now he looks back over all those years and wishes he'd prioritized differently—and invested in those relationships before he needed them to pay off for him.

Steve is hardly an isolated case. We all know people like him—and I think on some level many of us fear becoming that person in our later years. There's a reason that the film *It's a Wonderful Life* has been so resonant for decades: what matters most in the darkest hours of George Bailey's life are the many personal relationships he has invested in along the way. He recognizes, by the end of the film, that though he is poor, his life is rich in friendships. We all want to feel like George Bailey—but that simply isn't possible if we haven't done the work investing in those relationships with friends and family throughout our lives.

Each of us can point to one or two friendships we've unintentionally neglected when life got busy. You might be hoping that the bonds of your friendship are strong enough to endure such neglect, but that's seldom the case. Even the most committed friends will attempt to stay the course for only so long before they choose to invest their own time, energy, and friendship somewhere else. If they do, the loss will be yours.

People in their later years in life so often lament that they didn't keep in better touch with friends and relatives who once mattered profoundly to them. Life just seemed to get

in the way. The consequences of letting that happen, however, can be enormous. I've known too many people like
Steve, who have had to walk through a health struggle or a
divorce or a job loss alone—with nobody to provide a sound-
ing board or other means of support.

That can be the loneliest place in the world.

## The Risk of Sequencing Life Investments

One of the most common versions of this mistake that high-
potential young professionals make is believing that investments in life can be sequenced. The logic is, for example, "I
can invest in my career during the early years when our children are small and parenting isn't as critical. When our children are a bit older and begin to be interested in things that
adults are interested in, then I can lift my foot off my career
accelerator. That's when I'll focus on my family." Guess what.
By that time the game is already over. An investment in a
child needs to have been made long before then, to provide
him with the tools he needs to survive life's challenges—even
earlier than you might realize.

There's significant research emerging that demonstrates
just how important the earliest months of life are to the development of intellectual capacity. As recounted in our book
*Disrupting Class*, two researchers, Todd Risley and Betty
Hart, studied the effects of how parents talk to a child during
the first two and a half years of life. After meticulously observing and recording all of the interactions between parent
and child, they noticed that on average, parents speak 1,500

words per hour to their infant children. "Talkative" (often college-educated) parents spoke 2,100 words to their child, on average. By contrast, parents from less verbal (and often less-educated) backgrounds spoke only 600 per hour, on average. If you add that up over the first thirty months, the child of "talkative" parents heard an estimated 48 million words spoken, compared to the disadvantaged child, who heard only 13 million. The most important time for the children to hear the words, the research suggests, is the first year of life.

Risley and Hart's research followed the children they studied as they progressed through school. The number of words spoken to a child had a strong correlation between the number of words that they heard in their first thirty months and their performance on vocabulary and reading comprehension tests as they got older.

And it didn't matter that just any words were spoken to a child—the way a parent spoke to a child had a significant effect. The researchers observed two different types of conversations between parents and infants. One type they dubbed "business language"—such as, "Time for a nap," "Let's go for a ride," and "Finish your milk." Such conversations were simple and direct, not rich and complex. Risley and Hart concluded that these types of conversations had limited effect on cognitive development.

In contrast, when parents engaged in face-to-face conversation with the child—speaking in fully adult, sophisticated language as if the child could be part of a chatty, grown-up conversation—the impact on cognitive development was enormous. These richer interactions they called "language dancing." Language dancing is being chatty, thinking aloud, and commenting on what the child is doing and what the parent is doing or planning to do. "Do you want to wear the blue shirt or the red shirt today?" "Do you think it will rain today?" "Do you remember the time I put your bottle in the oven by mistake?" and so on. Language dancing involves talking to the child about "what if," and "do you remember," and "wouldn't it be nice if"—questions that invite the child to think deeply about what is happening around him. And it has a profound effect long before a parent might actually expect a child to understand what is being asked.

In short, when a parent engages in extra talk, many, many more of the synaptic pathways in the child's brain are exercised and refined. Synapses are the junctions in the brain where a signal is transmitted from one nerve cell to another. In simple terms, the more pathways that are created between synapses in the brain, the more efficiently connections are formed. This makes the subsequent patterns of thought easier and faster.

This matters. A child who has heard 48 million words in the first three years won't just have 3.7 times as many well-lubricated connections in its brain as a child who has heard only 13 million words. The effect on brain cells is exponential. Each brain cell can be connected to hundreds of other cells by as many as ten thousand synapses. That means children who have been exposed to extra talk have an almost incalculable cognitive advantage.

What's more, Risley and Hart's research suggests that "language dancing" is the key to this cognitive advantage—not income, ethnicity, or parents' education. "In other words," summarized Risley and Hart, "some working-poor people talked a lot to their kids and their kids did really well. Some affluent businesspeople talked very little to their kids and their kids did very poorly. . . . All the variation in outcomes was taken up by the amount of talking, in the family, to the babies before age three." A child who enters school with a strong vocabulary and strong cognitive abilities is likely to do well in school early on and continues to do well in the longer term.

It's mind-boggling to think that such a tiny investment has the potential for such enormous returns. Yet many parents think they can start focusing on their child's academic performance when they hit school. But by then, they've missed a huge window of opportunity to give their kid a leg up.

This is just one of the many ways in which investments in relationships with friends and family need to be made long, long before you'll see any sign that they are paying off.

If you defer investing your time and energy until you see that you need to, chances are it will already be too late. But as you are getting your career off the ground, you will be tempted to do exactly that: assume you can defer investing in your personal relationships. You cannot. The only way to have those relationships bear fruit in your life is to invest long before you need them.

~

*I genuinely believe that relationships with family and close friends are one of the greatest sources of happiness in life. It sounds simple, but like any important investment, these relationships need consistent attention and care. But there are two forces that will be constantly working against this happening. First, you'll be routinely tempted to invest your resources elsewhere—in things that will provide you with a more immediate payoff. And second, your family and friends rarely shout the loudest to demand your attention. They love you and they want to support your career, too. That can add up to neglecting the people you care about most in the world. The theory of good money, bad money explains that the clock of building a fulfilling relationship is ticking from the start. If you don't nurture and develop those relationships, they won't be there to support you if you find yourself traversing some of the more challenging stretches of life, or as one of the most important sources of happiness in your life.*

# CHAPTER SIX

# What Job Did You Hire
# That Milkshake For?

*Many products fail because companies develop them from the wrong perspective. Companies focus too much on what they want to sell their customers, rather than what those customers really need. What's missing is empathy: a deep understanding of what problems customers are trying to solve. The same is true in our relationships: we go into them thinking about what we want rather than what is important to the other person. Changing your perspective is a powerful way to deepen your relationships.*

~

## Doing the Job Right

Almost everyone has heard of the discount furniture store IKEA. It's been incredibly successful: the Swedish company has been rolling out its stores all over the world for the last forty years, and has global revenues in excess of 25 billion euros. The company's owner, Ingvar Kamprad, is one of the world's richest people. Not bad for a chain that sells inexpensive furniture you have to assemble yourself.

It's fascinating that in forty years, *nobody* has copied IKEA. Think about that for a second. Here is a business that has been immensely profitable for decades. IKEA doesn't have any big business secrets—any would-be competitor can walk through its stores, reverse-engineer its products, or copy its catalog . . . and yet nobody has done it.

Why is that?

IKEA's entire business model—the shopping experience, the layout of the store, the design of the products and the way they are packaged—is very different from the standard furniture store. Most retailers are organized around a customer segment, or a type of product. The customer base can then be divided up into target demographics, such as age, gender, education, or income level. In furniture retailing, over the years there have been stores such as Levitz Furniture, known for selling low-cost furniture to lower-income people. Or Ethan Allen, which made its name selling colonial-style furniture to wealthy people. And there are a host of other examples: stores organized around modern furniture for urban dwellers, stores that specialize in furniture for businesses, and so on.

IKEA has taken a totally different approach. Rather than organizing themselves around the characterization of particular customers or products, IKEA is structured around a job that customers periodically need to get done.

A job?

Through my research on innovation for the past two decades, my colleagues and I have developed a theory about this approach to marketing and product development, which we call "the job to be done." The insight behind this way of thinking is that what *causes* us to buy a product or service is that we actually hire products to do jobs for us.

What do I mean by that? We don't go through life conforming to particular demographic segments: nobody buys a product because he is an eighteen- to thirty-five-year-old white male getting a college degree. That may be *correlated* with a decision to buy this product instead of that one, but it doesn't *cause* us to buy anything. Instead, periodically we find that some job has arisen in our lives that we need to do, and we then find some way to get it done. If a company has developed a product or service to do the job well, we buy, or "hire" it, to do the job. If there isn't an existing product that does the job well, however, then we typically make something we already have, get it done as best we can, or develop a work-around. The mechanism that *causes* us to buy a product is "I have a job I need to get done, and this is going to help me do it."

My son Michael recently hired IKEA to do a job that had arisen in his life—which helped me understand why the company has been so successful. He was starting with a new employer in a new city after having lived on a student's budget for several years, and called me with a problem: "Dad,

I'm moving into my apartment tomorrow, and I need to get it furnished."

At this point, a name just jumped into our minds simultaneously: IKEA.

IKEA doesn't focus on selling a particular type of furniture to any particular demographically defined group of consumers. Rather, it focuses on a job that many consumers confront quite often as they establish themselves and their families in new surroundings: *I've got to get this place furnished tomorrow, because the next day I have to show up at work*. Competitors can copy IKEA's products. Competitors can even copy IKEA's layout. But what nobody has done is copy the way IKEA has integrated its products and its layout.

This thoughtful combination allows shoppers to quickly get everything done at once. It would seem counterintuitive to have the stores half an hour away, but this decision actually makes it much easier for people to get everything they need in one trip. It lets IKEA build a bigger store to ensure its furniture is always in stock. It has the space to build a supervised play area to keep the kids occupied—which is important because having a child tugging at your sleeve might cause you to forget something or rush through a decision. In case you get hungry, IKEA has a restaurant in the building so you don't have to leave. Its products are all flat-packed so that you can get them home quickly and easily in your own car. If you happen to buy so much that you can't fit it all in your car, IKEA has same-day delivery. And so on.

In fact, because IKEA does the job so well, many of its

customers have developed an intense loyalty to its products. My son Michael, for example, is one of IKEA's most enthusiastic customers because whenever he needs to furnish a new apartment or a room, he has learned that IKEA does the job perfectly. Whenever friends or family have the same job to do, Michael will cite chapter and verse on why IKEA does the job better than anyone else.

When a company understands the jobs that arise in people's lives, and then develops products and the accompanying experiences required in purchasing and using the product to do the job perfectly, it causes customers to instinctively "pull" the product into their lives whenever the job arises. But when a company simply makes a product that other companies also can make—and is a product that can do lots of jobs but none of them well—it will find that customers are rarely loyal to one product versus another. They will switch in a heartbeat when an alternative goes on sale.

## Cheaper? Chocolatier? Chunkier?

The job-to-be-done theory began to coalesce in a project that I worked on with some friends for one of the big fast-food restaurants. The company was trying to ramp up the sales of their milkshakes. The company had spent months studying the issue. They had brought customers in who fit the profile of the quintessential milkshake consumer and peppered them with questions: "Can you tell us how we can improve our milkshake so you'd buy more of them? Do you want it chocolatier?

Cheaper? Chunkier?" The company would take all this feedback, then go off and improve the milkshake on those dimensions. They worked and worked on making the milkshake better as a result—but these improvements had no impact on sales or profits whatsoever. The company was stumped.

My colleague Bob Moesta then offered to bring a completely different perspective to the milkshake problem: "I wonder what job arises in people's lives that causes them to come to this restaurant to 'hire' a milkshake?"

That was an interesting way to think about the problem. So they stood in a restaurant hours on end, taking very careful data: What time did people buy these milkshakes? What were they wearing? Were they alone? Did they buy other food with it? Did they eat it in the restaurant or drive off with it?

Surprisingly, it turned out that nearly half of the milkshakes were sold in the early morning. The people who bought those morning milkshakes were almost always alone; it was the only thing they bought; and almost all of them got in a car and drove off with it.

To figure out what job they were hiring that milkshake to do, we came back another morning and stood outside the restaurant so that we could confront these folks as they left, milkshake in hand. As they emerged and, in language that they could understand, we essentially asked each of them, "Excuse me. Can you help me understand what job you are trying to do with that milkshake?" When they'd struggle to answer this question, we'd help them by asking, "Well, think about the last time you were in this same situation, needing to get the same job done—but you didn't come here to hire that milkshake. What did you hire?" The answers were enlightening: Bananas. Doughnuts. Bagels. Candy bars. But the milkshake was clearly their favorite.

As we put all the answers together, it became clear that the early-morning customers all had the same job to do: they had a long and boring ride to work. They needed something to do while driving to keep the commute interesting. They weren't really hungry yet, but they knew that in a couple of hours, they'd face a midmorning stomach rumbling. "What else do I hire to do this job?" one mused. "I hire bananas sometimes. But take my word for it: don't do bananas. They are gone too quickly—and you'll be hungry again by midmorning." Some people complained that doughnuts were too crumbly and left their fingers sticky, making a mess on their clothes and the steering wheel as they tried to eat and drive. A common complaint about hiring bagels for this job was that they were dry and tasteless—forcing people to drive their cars with their knees while they spread cream cheese and jam on the bagels. Another commuter used our language and confessed, "One time I hired a Snickers bar. But I felt so guilty about eating candy for breakfast that I never did it again."

But a milkshake? It was the best of the lot. It took a long time to finish a thick milkshake with that thin straw. And it was substantial enough to ward off the looming midmorning hunger attack. One commuter effused, "This milkshake. It is so thick! It easily takes me twenty minutes to suck it up through that little straw. Who cares what the ingredients are—I don't. All I know is that I'm full all morning. And it fits right here in my cup holder"—as he held up his empty hand.

It turns out that the milkshake does the job better than any of the competitors—which, in the customers' minds, are not just milkshakes from other chains but bananas, bagels, doughnuts, breakfast bars, smoothies, coffee, and so on.

That was a breakthrough insight for the fast-food chain— but the breakthroughs were not over yet. We discovered that in the afternoon and evening, the same product was hired for a fundamentally different job. Instead of commuters, the people who were coming in to buy milkshakes in the after- noon and evening were typically fathers—fathers who had had to say "no" to their children about any number of things all week long. No new toy. No, they can't stay up late. No, they can't have a puppy.

I recognized that I had been one of those dads, more times than I could remember, and I had the same job to do when I was in that situation. I'd been looking for something innocuous to which I could say "yes," to make me feel like a kind and loving father. So I'm standing there in line with my son and I order my meal. Then my son Spencer orders his meal—and he pauses to look up at me like only a son can, and asks, "Dad, can I have a milkshake, too?" And the moment has arrived when I can say "yes" to my son and feel good about myself. I reach down, put my hand on his shoul- der, and say, "Of course, Spence, you can have a milkshake."

Turns out, the milkshakes didn't do that particular job at all well. When we watched those father-son tables, the dads, like me, finished their meal first. The son would then finish his. And then he would pick up that thick milkshake—and it took him forever to suck it up that thin little straw.

Dads didn't hire the milkshake to keep their son entertained for a long time; they hired it to be nice. They'd patiently wait while their son struggled to make progress on the shake. But after a while, they'd grow impatient. "Look, son, I'm sorry, but we don't have all night . . ." They'd clean up their table and the milkshake would get thrown away half finished.

If our fast-food chain asked me, "So, Clay . . . how can we improve the milkshake so that you'll buy more of them? Thicker? Sweeter? Bigger?" I wouldn't know what to say, because I hire it for two fundamentally different jobs. Then, when they averaged up the responses of the key forty-five- to sixty-five-year-old demographic segment that has the highest proclivity to buy milkshakes, it would guide them to develop a one-size-fits-none product that doesn't do either job well.

On the other hand, if you understand that there are two different jobs that the milkshake is being hired to do, it becomes obvious how to improve the shake. The morning job needs a more viscous milkshake, which takes even longer to suck up. You might add in chunks of fruit—but not to make it healthy, because that's not the reason it's being hired. It's being hired by morning customers to keep their commute interesting. The unexpected pieces of fruit would do just that. And, finally, you'd wheel the dispensing machine out from behind the counter to the front, and install a prepaid swipecard, so that commuters could run in, gas up, and go—and never get caught in a line.

The afternoon make-me-feel-good-about-being-a-parent job is fundamentally different. Maybe the afternoon milkshake should come in half sizes; be less thick so it could be finished more quickly; and so on.

There is no one right answer for all circumstances. You have to start by understanding the job the customer is trying to have done.

## The Job of Keeping Mom and Dad Happy

Not long ago, an inventor approached a New Hampshire company called the Big Idea Group with an idea for a card game he had created. The chief executive of BIG, Mike Collins, didn't think the game would sell. But instead of sending the inventor packing, he asked him, "What caused you to develop this game?" Rather than justifying the game he developed, the inventor's answer identified a problem that arose repeatedly in his life: "I have three young children and a demanding job. By the time I get home from work and we finish dinner, it's eight o'clock and the kids need to go to bed. But we haven't had any fun together. What am I going to do? Set up Monopoly or Risk? I need some fun games that we can set up, play, and put away in fifteen minutes."

Aha! This job arose in this man's life at least five days a week.

Though Collins felt that the father's game was only mediocre, the valuable insight was the job itself. Millions of busy parents think about the same thing every evening. The identification of the job the inventor was trying to do led to a very successful line called "12 Minute Games." It was only through living with a real problem that the dad had the insight to create a line of games that do a job important to millions of people.

Every successful product or service, either explicitly or implicitly, was structured around a job to be done. Addressing a job is the causal mechanism behind a purchase. If someone develops a product that is interesting, but which doesn't intuitively map in customers' minds on a job that they are trying to do, that product will struggle to succeed—unless the product is adapted and repositioned on an important job.

The makers of V8 vegetable juice used this theory of jobs to grow their business in a stunning way, as recounted by one of their executives who attended one of our executive education programs about four years ago. For years, the advertising campaign for V8, a juice that promises the nutrients of eight different vegetables, had used the refrain, "Wow, I could've had a V8!" It was sold as an alternative to refreshing drinks, like apple juice, soft drinks, Gatorade, and so on. But only a smattering of customers actually preferred V8, when compared to these other products.

After reading one of the papers my colleagues and I had written about the virtues of defining products and market segments in terms of jobs to be done, they realized that there was another job in their part of the world, in which the V8 was far better equipped to compete: providing vegetables' nutrients. Most of us promised our mothers when we left home that we would eat vegetables in order to maintain our health. But hiring fresh vegetables to do the job entails peeling, slicing, cubing, and shredding, and then boiling, baking, or otherwise preparing vegetables—all so that we can eat a food that most of us don't really like.

"Or," the executive recalled, "the customers could say, 'I could drink a V8, and get all the nutrition that I promised Mom that I'd get, but with a fraction of the effort and time!'" Once the makers of V8 had that realization, the ad campaign changed to focus on how the drink provided the required daily vegetable servings. It worked. The executive recounted that V8 quadrupled its revenues within a year of their decision to position it on a different job, allowing it to compete against its inconvenient competitors: vegetables.

## Hiring School for a Job

Without realizing it, we use this job-to-be-done mind-set in our interactions with people all the time. To illustrate, I'll summarize a study we did to understand why our schools in America struggle to improve—a study that culminated in our book *Disrupting Class*. One of the primary puzzles in the research was why so many of our schoolchildren just seem unmotivated to learn. We bring technology, special education, amusement, field trips, and many other improvements in the way we teach, and little seems to make a difference.

What's going on? The answer lies in understanding what jobs arise in the lives of students that schools might be hired to solve.

The conclusion we reached was that going to school is not a job that children are trying to get done. It is something that a child might hire to do the job, but it isn't *the* job itself. The two fundamental jobs that children need to do are to feel successful and to have friends—every day. Sure, they could hire school to get these jobs done. Some achieve success and friends in the classroom, the band, the math club, or the basketball team. But to feel successful and have friends, they could also drop out of school and join a gang, or buy a car and cruise the streets. Viewed from the perspective of jobs, it becomes very clear that schools don't often do these jobs well at all—in fact, all too often, schools are structured to help most students feel like failures. We had assumed going in that those who succeed at school do so because they are motivated. But we concluded that all students are similarly motivated—to succeed. The problem is, only a fraction of students feel successful through school.

Indeed, we learned that just as the fast-food restaurant had been improving the milkshake on dimensions of improvement irrelevant to the jobs that customers were trying to do, our schools were improving themselves on dimensions of improvement irrelevant to the job that students are trying to do. There is no way that we can motivate children to work harder in class by *convincing* them that they *should* do this. Rather, we need to offer children experiences in school that help them do these jobs—to feel successful and do it with friends.

Schools that have designed their curriculum so that students feel success every day see rates of dropping out and absenteeism fall to nearly zero. When structured to do the job of success, students eagerly master difficult material—because in doing so, they are getting the job done.

## What Job Are You Being Hired For?

If you work to understand what job you are being hired to do, both professionally and in your personal life, the payoff will be enormous. In fact, it is here that this theory yields the most insight, simply because one of the most important jobs you'll ever be hired to do is to be a spouse. Getting this right, I believe, is critical to sustaining a happy marriage.

Just as we learned in our research about the jobs that school students are trying to do, I'll describe in the subsequent pages how this framing can impact our marriages and relationships. To economize on words, I've framed the first person with masculine pronouns and adjectives, and used feminine words for the spouse. But they can be swapped around without changing the meaning at all—the concepts apply equally to everyone.

Like those milkshake buyers, you and your wife can't always articulate what the fundamental jobs are that *you each* are personally trying to do, let alone articulate the fundamental jobs that your wife has, for which she might hire a husband to get done. Understanding the job requires the critical ingredients of intuition and empathy. You have to be able to put yourself not just in her shoes, but her chair—and indeed, her life. More important, the jobs that your spouse is trying to do are often *very* different from the jobs that you *think* she should want to do.

Ironically, it is for this reason that many unhappy mar-riages are often built upon selflessness. But the selflessness is based on the partners giving each other things that they want to give, and which they have decided that their partner ought to want—as in, "Honey, believe me, you are going to love this Iridium wireless telephone!"

It's easy for any of us to make assumptions about what our spouse might want, rather than work hard to understand the job to be done in our spouse's life. Let me share an ex-ample from Scott, a friend of mine with three children un-der the age of five. One day recently, Scott came home from work to find a highly unusual scene—the breakfast dishes still on the table and dinner not started. His instant reaction was that his wife, Barbara, had had a tough day and needed a hand. Without a word, he rolled up his sleeves, cleaned up the breakfast dishes, and started dinner. Partway through, Barbara disappeared. But Scott kept on, making dinner for the kids. He had just started feeding them when he suddenly wondered, where's Barbara? Tired, but feeling pretty good about himself, he went upstairs to try to figure out where she was. He found her alone in their bedroom. He expected to be thanked for doing all that at the end of an exhausting day at work. But instead Barbara was *very* upset—at him.

He was shocked. He had just done all this for *her*. What had he done wrong?

"How could you ignore me after I've had such a difficult day?" Barbara asked.

"You think that I've ignored you?" Scott responded. "I finished the breakfast dishes, cleaned up the kitchen, fixed dinner, and am partway through feeding our children. How in the world can you think I've ignored you?"

Just then, it became clear to Scott what had happened. Indeed, what he did was important to get done, and he was trying to be selfless in giving Barbara exactly what *he* thought she needed. Barbara explained, however, that the day hadn't been difficult because of the chores. It was difficult because she had spent hours and hours with small, demanding children, and she hadn't spoken to another adult all day. What she needed most at that time was a real conversation with an adult who cared about her. By doing what he did, he only made Barbara feel guilty and angry about her frustration.

Interactions like those between Scott and Barbara occur thousands of times every day in households around the world. We project what we want and assume that it's also what our spouse wants. Scott probably wished he had helping hands to get through his tough day at work, so that's what he offered Barbara when he got home. It's so easy to mean well but get it wrong. A husband may be convinced that he is the selfless one, and also convinced that his wife is being self-centered because she doesn't even notice everything he is giving her—and vice versa. This is exactly the interaction between the customers and the marketers of so many companies, too.

Yes, we can do all kinds of things for our spouse, but if we are not focused on the jobs she most needs doing, we will reap frustration and confusion in our search for happiness in that relationship. Our effort is misplaced—we are just making a chocolatier milkshake. This may be the single hardest thing to get right in a marriage. Even with good intentions and deep love, we can fundamentally misunderstand each other. We get caught up in the day-to-day chores of our lives. Our communication ends up focusing only on who is doing what. We assume things.

I suspect that if we studied marriage from the job-to-be-done lens, we would find that the husbands and wives who are most loyal to each other are those who have figured out the jobs that their partner needs to be done—and then they do the job reliably and well. I know for me, this has a profound effect. By working to truly understand the job she needs done, and doing it well, I can cause myself to fall more deeply in love with my spouse, and, I hope, her with me. Divorce, on the other hand, often has its roots when one frames marriage only in terms of whether she is giving me what I want. If she isn't, then I dispense with her, and find someone else who will.

## Sacrifice and Commitment

This may sound counterintuitive, but I deeply believe that the path to happiness in a relationship is not just about finding someone who you think is going to make you happy. Rather, the reverse is equally true: the path to happiness is about finding someone who you want to make happy, someone whose happiness is worth devoting yourself to. If what causes us to fall deeply in love is mutually understanding and then doing each other's job to be done, then I have observed that what *cements* that commitment is the extent to which I sacrifice myself to help *her* succeed and for *her* to be happy.

This principle—that sacrifice deepens our commitment—doesn't just work in marriages. It applies to members of our family and close friends, as well as organizations and even cultures and nations.

For illustration, let me offer you the example of the U.S. Marines, who achieve a deep sense of attachment to the organization, to their peers, and to their country. But not because it is fun—surviving Marine Corps training alone may be one of the hardest challenges of many young Marines' lives to that point. The job almost kills them. They sacrifice so much for the corps and their fellow Marines. But you can routinely see "Semper Fi"—Always Faithful—bumper stickers on cars all over America.

Our daughter, Annie, also experienced this while serving as a missionary for our church in Mongolia. When she first found out that she was going there, her younger brother, Spence, got her a travel guide. It offered a bleak picture: "This is a great country. But we don't think you should go in the winter, because it gets down to 65 degrees below zero. And, actually, we don't think you should go in the summer, either: it gets up to 125 degrees Fahrenheit. But especially don't go in the spring: sand storms erupt on the Gobi Desert. If you get caught in one, it will strip the paint off your car and the skin off your body. Other than this, though, you will love your time in this beautiful nation!"

That didn't look too promising, but we shipped her off to Mongolia nonetheless. As the book predicted, it was a brutal experience at times; we now understand why Genghis Khan was so eager to migrate south. It is one tough place. Because of the climate, there are just a few places where grains and vegetables can grow. As a result the diet—even snacks—is composed almost entirely of animal products, from horses, sheep, yaks, and goats. Yet Annie persisted for the full eighteen months of her assignment there, teaching and trying to help everyone whom she met there become a better person. It was one of the hardest things she's done in her life.

But you know what? Annie left half of her heart with the Mongolian people forever—and it greatly strengthened her commitment to our church.

I feel exactly the same way about Korea and the remarkable Korean people because I served as a young missionary in Korea back when it was one of the poorest countries in Asia. Neither Annie nor I feel this intense attachment to the people of those countries or to our church because our work there was easy—it's the opposite. We feel this way because we gave so much of ourselves.

Given that sacrifice deepens our commitment, it's important to ensure that what we sacrifice for is *worthy* of that commitment, as the church was for me and Annie. Perhaps nothing deserves sacrifice more than family—and not just that others should sacrifice for you, but that you should sacrifice for your family, too. I believe it is an essential foundation to deep friendships and fulfilling, happy families and marriages.

One of the first times I observed this was in the family of Edward and Joan Quinn, my parents-in-law. My wife, Christine, is the oldest of twelve children, raised in a family in which there was little money, a lot of love, and a compelling need to help each other succeed. They had to give up a lot for each other; there was no space for selfishness. I know innumerable families, but I have never known any whose loyalty for each other surpasses this family. If anything ever begins to go amiss in the life of any member of this now even larger family, everyone—literally everyone—is standing in line the next day, not simply offering help, but actively searching for ways to help.

I have experienced this within my own life, too. I was a student in England when my father learned that he had cancer—and within a couple of months, it was clear that he wasn't getting better. I returned home to help my mother and siblings take care of him. I didn't think twice about doing this; it was just what needed to be done.

My dad had worked in the same department store, ZCMI, for most of his life. When we were kids, every Saturday we would go down to the store and help him do his job—or at least he made us feel as though we were helping him by stocking shelves, turning the labels carefully forward, and weighing small bags of nuts and spices, even if we only slowed him down. From helping him over the years, we learned a lot about his job.

When my dad eventually got so sick that he couldn't keep working, I offered to go to work in his place. One week, I was a student at Oxford having a heady academic experience. The next, I was back home stocking department store shelves with Christmas holiday merchandise.

Now you might think that, in hindsight, I could have resented what happened. And yet I consider those months to be among the happiest times I ever spent with my dad and my family. As I reflect back on why, it's *because* I put my whole life on hold for them.

~

*It's natural to want the people you love to be happy. What can often be difficult is understanding what your role is in that. Thinking about your relationships from the perspective of the* job to be done *is the best way to understand what's important to the people who mean the most to you. It allows you to develop true empathy. Asking yourself "What job does my spouse most need me to do?" gives you the ability to think about it in the right unit of analysis. When you approach your relationships from this perspective, the answers will become much more clear than they would by simply speculating about what might be the right thing to do.*

*But you have to go beyond understanding what job your spouse needs you to do. You have to do that job. You'll have to devote your time and energy to the effort, be willing to suppress your own priorities and desires, and focus on doing what is required to make the other person happy. Nor should we be timid in giving our children and our spouses the same opportunities to give of themselves to others. You might think this approach would actually cause resentment in relationships because one person is so clearly giving up something for the other. But I have found that it has the opposite effect. In sacrificing for something worthwhile, you deeply strengthen your commitment to it.*

# CHAPTER SEVEN

# Sailing Your Kids on Theseus's Ship

*We all recognize the importance of giving our kids the best opportunities. Each new generation of parents seems to focus even more on creating possibilities for their children that they themselves never had. With the best of intentions, we hand our children off to a myriad of coaches and tutors to provide them with enriching experiences—thinking that will best prepare our kids for the future. But helping our children in this way can come at a high cost.*

∿

## The Greek Tragedy of Outsourcing

Over the past two decades, Dell has been one of the world's most successful PC manufacturers. Few people realize, however, that one of the reasons for Dell's success was a Taiwanese component supplier by the name of Asus.

Dell hit its stride in the early 1990s—using several beacons to guide its growth. First, its business model was disruptive: it started making simple entry-level computers at very low costs, because they sold largely by mail or over the Web. It then moved up-market, making a sequence of higher- and higher-performing computers. Second, its products were modular—allowing its customers to customize their own computers by choosing what components they wanted in their machines. Dell would then assemble and ship them within forty-eight hours—an impressive achievement. And third, Dell tried to use its capital more and more efficiently, wringing more and more sales and profits per dollar of its assets—something Wall Street applauded. These three strategic beacons helped Dell succeed in quite an extraordinary way.

Interestingly, it was actually Taiwan-based Asus that enabled Dell to pull this off. Like Dell, Asus started at the low end providing simple, reliable circuits for Dell—at a lower price than what Dell could do itself.

In that context, Asus came to Dell with an interesting proposition: "We've done a good job making these little circuits for you. Let us supply the motherboards for your computers, too. Making motherboards isn't *your* competence—it's *ours*. And we can make them for a 20 percent lower cost." The Dell analysts realized that not only could Asus do it cheaper but it would also allow Dell to erase all the motherboard-related manufacturing assets from its balance sheet.

Wall Street analysts hawkishly monitor financial metrics and ratios that track the "efficiency" of capital used in a business. One particularly common one is RONA, or Return on Net Assets. In manufacturing businesses, this is calculated by dividing a company's income by its net assets. Hence, a company can be judged as being more profitable either by adding income to the numerator, or by reducing the assets in the denominator. Driving the numerator up is harder, because it entails selling more products. Driving the denominator down is often easier—because you can just opt to outsource. The higher the ratio, the more efficient a business is judged to be in using its capital. Asus's proposal made sense. If Dell could outsource some of its assets but still be able to sell its customers the same products, then it would improve its RONA, making Wall Street happy. "Gosh, that would be a great idea," Dell said to Asus. "You can produce our motherboards." Funny enough, the agreement made Asus look better to investors, too; it was increasing its sales with the use of its existing assets. Both companies seemed better off.

After it had reorganized to accommodate this arrangement, Asus came to Dell and said, "We've done a good job fabricating these motherboards for you. Why don't you let us assemble the whole computer for you, too? Assembling those products is not what's made you successful. We can take all the remaining manufacturing assets off your balance sheet, and we can do it all for 20 percent less."

The Dell analysts realized that this, too, was a win-win. As Asus took on the additional activity, Asus's RONA increased as the numerator of the ratio—profits—got bigger. Shedding manufacturing processes also increased Dell's RONA—it didn't change the revenue line, but driving out those assets from its balance sheet improved the denominator of the ratio.

That process continued as Dell outsourced the management of its supply chain, and then the design of its computers themselves. Dell essentially outsourced everything inside its personal-computer business—everything except its brand—to Asus. Dell's RONA became *very* high, as it had very few assets left in the consumer part of its business.

Then, in 2005, Asus announced the creation of its own brand of computers. In this Greek-tragedy tale, Asus had taken everything it had learned from Dell and applied it for itself. It started at the simplest of activities in the value chain, then, decision by decision, every time that Dell outsourced the next lowest-value-adding of the remaining activities in its business, Asus added a higher value-adding activity to its business.

All along, the numbers had looked good to Dell. But what the numbers had not shown was the impact these decisions would have on Dell's future. Dell started out as one of the most exciting computer companies around, but over the years, it has slowly outsourced its way to mediocrity in the consumer business. Dell doesn't build those computers. It doesn't ship those computers. It doesn't service those computers. It simply allows companies in Taiwan to put the name "Dell" on the machines.

To be fair to Dell, it has successfully moved into the higher-profit server business, which is prospering. But on the consumer side, Dell outsourced something far more critical than it might have realized.

## Understand Your Capabilities

You can tell from this story that there's a danger to outsourcing. Clearly, if Dell's leadership had known what the outcome would be from taking the approach they did, they would have been much more hesitant to accept Asus's overtures. But how *could* they have known?

The answer lies in understanding the concept of "capabilities." You need to understand what capabilities are, and which of them will be critical to the future, to know which capabilities are important to keep in-house and which matter less.

What do I mean by this?

When you boil it down, the factors that determine what a company can and cannot do—its capabilities—fall into one of three buckets: resources, processes, and priorities. These offer an accurate snapshot of a company at any given time, because they are mutually exclusive (a part of a business cannot fit into more than one of the categories) and are collectively exhaustive (together, the three categories account for everything inside of the business). Together, these capabilities are crucial in order to assess what a company can and, perhaps more important, cannot accomplish.

Capabilities are dynamic and built over time; no company starts out with its capabilities fully developed. The most tangible of the three factors is *resources*, which include people, equipment, technology, product designs, brands, information, cash, and relationships with suppliers, distributors, and customers. Resources are usually people or things— they can be hired and fired, bought and sold, depreciated or built. Many resources are visible and often are measurable, so managers can readily assess their value. Most people might think that resources are what make a business successful.

But resources are only one of three critical factors driving a business. Organizations create value as employees transform resources into products and services of greater worth. The ways in which those employees interact, coordinate, communicate, and make decisions are known as *processes*. These enable the resources to solve more and more complicated problems.

Processes include the ways that products are developed and made, and the methods by which market research, budgeting, employee development, compensation, and resource allocation are accomplished. Unlike resources, which are often easily seen and measured, processes can't be seen on a balance sheet.

If a company has strong processes in place, managers have flexibility about which employees they put on which assignments—because the process will work regardless of who performs it. Take, for example, consulting firm McKinsey, which is hired to help companies around the world. McKinsey's processes are so pervasive that consultants from very different backgrounds and training can be "plugged" into the processes by which they habitually do their work— with confidence that they will deliver the needed results.

The third—and perhaps most significant—capability is an organization's *priorities*. This set of factors defines how a company makes decisions; it can give clear guidance about what a company is likely to invest in, and what it will not. Employees at every level will make prioritization decisions—what they will focus on today, and what they'll put at the bottom of their list.

Managers can't be there to watch over every decision as a company gets bigger. That's why the larger and more complex a company becomes, the more important it is for senior managers to ensure employees make, by themselves, prioritization decisions that are consistent with the strategic direction and the business model of the company. It means that successful senior executives need to spend a lot of time articulating clear, consistent priorities that are broadly understood throughout the organization. Over time, a company's priorities must be in sync with how the company makes money, because employees *must* prioritize those things that support the company's strategy, if the company is to survive. Otherwise the decisions they make will be in conflict with the foundation of the business.

## Never Outsource the Future

Like Dell, companies in the pharmaceutical, automobile, oil, information technology, semiconductor, and many other industries have increasingly pursued outsourcing without considering the importance of future capabilities. They are encouraged to do this by financiers, consultants, and academics—they see how quickly and easily they can reap the benefits of outsourcing, and don't see the cost of losing the capabilities that they forgo in doing so. They risk creating their own version of Asus.

The history of outsourcing in the American semiconductor industry, for example, chronicles the woes that betide companies that blindly adhere to outsourcing. At the outset, it made all the sense in the world to outsource the simplest of the steps entailed in making semiconductor products to Chinese and Taiwanese suppliers. The American semiconductor companies thought they were safe, as they retained the more complex and profitable steps, such as product design.

But although the Asian suppliers started out by assembling only the simplest of products, they didn't want to stay there. It was low-cost work, and almost anyone could do it. They knew that they would be vulnerable to losing that work to an even lower-cost assembler. So those Asian suppliers strove to keep moving up-market, fabricating and assembling ever more sophisticated products. Now the suppliers in Taiwan, Korea, Singapore, and China have become capable of making products and components that their American customers, who outsourced to these suppliers in the first place, could no longer hope to ever make.

The tables truly have turned. At the beginning, American companies outsourced simple things to drive costs down and get assets off their balance sheets. As is often the case, each of the decisions by themselves seemed to make sense. Now, however, they must outsource sophisticated products because they can no longer make them.

The theory of capabilities gives companies the framework to determine when outsourcing makes sense, and when it does not. There are two important considerations. First, you must take a *dynamic* view of your suppliers' capabilities. Assume that they can and will change. You should not focus on what the suppliers are doing now, but, rather, focus on what they are striving to be able to do in the future. Second, and most critical of all: figure out what capabilities you will need to succeed in the future. These *must* stay in-house—otherwise, you are handing over the future of your business. Understanding the power and importance of capabilities can make the difference between a good CEO and a mediocre one.

## What Your Child Can and Cannot Do

Whether we realize it or not, we are assessing capabilities all around us every day. We assess everything about our organizations; our bosses, our colleagues and peers, and our employees. We assess our competitors. But if I asked you to turn that lens closer to home, could you do it? What are your capabilities? What about your family's? It may seem funny to think of ourselves as a composite of resources, processes, and priorities, just like a business. But it's an insightful way to assess what we are able to accomplish in our own lives—and what might be out of our reach. I'll bet if you listed your own capabilities, there are some that you know are real strengths and assets. But every one of us has a few areas that we wish were stronger—capabilities you would go back in time and develop better if you could.

Unfortunately, none of us has the luxury of doing so. Just as Dell can't wind back the clock on the decisions it made to

outsource its capabilities, we can't go back to our youth to figure out ways to develop the capabilities we wish we had. But,
as parents, we do have the opportunity to help our children
get it right. The *Resources, Processes, and Priorities* model of
capabilities can help us gauge what our children will need to
be able to do, given the types of challenges and problems that
we know they will confront in their future.

The first of the factors that determine what a child can
and cannot do is his resources. These include the financial and
material resources he has been given or has earned, his time
and energy, what he knows, what his talents are, what relationships he has built, and what he has learned from the past.

The second group of factors that determine a child's capabilities are processes. Processes are what your child does
with the resources he has, to accomplish and create new
things for himself. Just as within a business, they are relatively intangible, but are a large part of what makes each
child unique. These include the way he thinks, how he asks
insightful questions, how and whether he can solve problems
of various types, how he works with others, and so on.

Let me give you some examples to highlight the difference
between the resources and processes of a child. Take a young
man sitting in class. Teachers and scholars can create knowledge, and our young man can sit in class and passively absorb
the knowledge that others have created. That knowledge now
becomes a resource for him; he might use it to get a better
score on a test that simply measures how much information he
has acquired. But it doesn't necessarily mean he has acquired
the ability to *create* new knowledge. If he were able to take the

information he absorbed in class and use it to, say, create an application for a tablet computer, like an iPad, or conduct his own scientific experiment—*that* capability is a process.

If those describe the resources and processes of a child, the final capability is the child's personal priorities. They're not that dissimilar from the priorities we have in our own lives: school, sports, family, work, and faith are all examples. Priorities determine how a child will make decisions in his life—which things in his mind and life he will put to the top of the list, which he will procrastinate doing, and which he will have no interest in doing at all.

To understand how all three work together, let's continue the example of a child developing an iPad app. If your child has a computer on which to program, and knowledge of how to program an iPad app, he has resources. The way in which he pulls these resources together to create something novel, something that he hasn't been taught explicitly how to do, to learn as he goes along—these are his processes. And the desire he has to spend his precious free time creating the app, the problem he cares about enough to create the app to solve, the idea of creating something unique, or the fact that he cares that his friends will be impressed—those are the priorities leading him to do it. Resources are *what* he uses to do it, processes are *how* he does it, and priorities are *why* he does it.

## The Greek Tragedy—Inside Our Families

I worry *a lot* that many, many parents are doing to their children what Dell did to its personal-computing business—

removing the circumstances in which they can develop processes. As a general rule, in prosperous societies we have been outsourcing more and more of the work that, a generation ago, was done "internally" in the home. It sounds almost quaint by comparison to life now, but in the modest neighborhood in which I grew up, there was a lot of work going on in our homes. We had gardens and fruit trees; we grew a lot of what we ate. We had to preserve much of what we grew so we could eat it during the winter and spring. Our mothers made much of the clothing that we wore; and in the absence of wrinkle-free fabrics, we had to spend hours and hours washing and ironing our clothes. The idea that one might hire someone else to mow the lawn and shovel the snow at your home—it just never happened. There was so much work going on that children essentially worked for their parents.

Step by step, over the past fifty years, it has become cheaper and easier to outsource this work to professionals. Now the only work being done in many of our homes is a periodic cleanup of the mess that we make. In the absence of work, we've created a generation of parents who selflessly devote themselves to providing their children with enriching experiences—so-called soccer moms, a term that wasn't even part of the American lexicon until fifteen years ago. They lovingly cart children around to soccer, lacrosse, basketball, football, hockey, and baseball teams; dance, gymnastics, music, and Chinese lessons; send them on a semester abroad to London; and to so many camps that many children don't even have the time to get a part-time job in the summer. Taken individually, each of these can be a wonderful chance for a child to develop, and an excellent substitute for all the work that used to take place around the home. Kids can learn to overcome difficult challenges, take on responsibility, become good team players. They're opportunities to develop the critical processes that kids will need to succeed later in life.

Too often, however, parents foist all these experiences on their children without that in mind. Now, on one hand, exposing them to lots of activities is commendable. You want to help your kids discover something that they truly enjoy doing, and it's actually critical for them to find something that will motivate them to develop their own processes.

But that's not always the impetus of parents imposing these activities on their children's lives. Parents have their own job to be done, and it can overshadow the desire to help their children develop processes. They have a job of wanting to feel like a good parent: see all the opportunities I'm providing for my child? Or parents, often with their heart in the right place, project their own hopes and dreams onto their children.

When these other intentions start creeping in, and parents seem to be carting their children around to an endless array of activities in which the kids are not truly engaged, it should start to raise red flags. Are the children developing from these experiences the deep, important processes such as teamwork, entrepreneurship, and learning the value of preparation? Or are they just going along for the ride? When we so heavily focus on providing our children with resources, we need to ask ourselves a new set of questions: Has my child developed the skill to develop better skills? The knowledge to develop deeper knowledge? The experience to learn from his experiences? These are the critical differences between resources and processes in our children's minds and hearts—and, I fear, the unanticipated residual of outsourcing.

When Dell outsourced a part of its business to Asus, Dell gave Asus targets it needed to hit, and problems that it needed to solve. Asus then developed the processes for doing the work—even as Dell's processes for doing the same work atrophied. Asus honed and expanded those processes so that it could complete more and more sophisticated work. Dell didn't see that as it was focusing so heavily on resources and reducing its crucial processes, that it was actually undermining its future competitiveness.

Many parents are making the same mistake, flooding their children with resources—knowledge, skills, and experiences. And just as with Dell, each of the decisions to do so seems to make sense. We want our kids to get ahead, and believe that the opportunities and experiences we have provided for them will help them do exactly that. But the nature of these activities—experiences in which they're not deeply engaged and that don't really challenge them to do hard things—denies our children the opportunity to develop the processes they'll need to succeed in the future.

## What My Parents Didn't Do for Me

The end result of these good intentions for our children is that too few reach adulthood having been given the opportunity to shoulder onerous responsibility and solve complicated problems for themselves and for others. Self-esteem—the sense that "I'm not afraid to confront this problem and I think I can solve it"—doesn't come from abundant resources. Rather, self-esteem comes from achieving something important when it's hard to do.

At the time of this writing and for the first time in modern economics, unemployment among young men is higher than almost any other group in America and, indeed, this is true of many developed countries around the world. How could this be? Reasonable people can debate whether this is the result of the economic policies of past decades, but I think another factor is contributing to this situation. I worry that an entire generation has reached adulthood without the capabilities—particularly the processes—that translate into employment. We have outsourced the work from our homes, and we've allowed the vacuum to be filled with activities that don't challenge or engage our kids. By sheltering children from the problems that arise in life, we have inadvertently denied this generation the ability to develop the processes and priorities it needs to succeed.

I'm not advocating throwing kids straight into the deep end to see whether they can swim. Instead, it's a case of starting early to find simple problems for them to solve on their own, problems that can help them build their processes—and a healthy self-esteem. As I look back on my own life, I recognize that some of the greatest gifts I received from my parents stemmed not from what they did for me—but rather from what they *didn't* do for me. One such example: my mother never mended my clothes. I remember going to her when I was in the early grades of elementary school, with holes in both socks of my favorite pair. My mom had just had her sixth child and was deeply involved in our church activities. She was very, very busy. Our family had no extra money anywhere, so buying new socks was just out of the question. So she told me to go string thread through a needle, and to come back when I had done it. That accomplished—it took me about ten minutes, whereas I'm sure she could have done it in ten seconds—she took one of the socks and showed me how to run the needle in and out around the periphery of the hole, rather than back and forth across the hole, and then simply to draw the hole closed. This took her about thirty seconds. Finally, she showed me how to cut and knot the thread. She then handed me the second sock, and went on her way.

A year or so later—I probably was in third grade—I fell down on the playground at school and ripped my Levi's. This was serious, because I had the standard family ration of two pairs of school trousers. So I took them to my mom and asked if she could repair them. She showed me how to set up and operate her sewing machine, including switching it to a zigzag stitch; gave me an idea or two about how she might try to repair it if it were she who was going to do the repair, and then went on her way. I sat there clueless at first, but eventually figured it out.

Although in retrospect these were very simple things, they represent a defining point in my life. They helped me to learn that I should solve my own problems whenever possible; they gave me the confidence that I could solve my own problems; and they helped me experience pride in that achievement. It's funny, but every time I put those socks on until they were threadbare, I looked at that repair in the toe and thought, "I did that." I have no memory now of what the repair to the knee of those Levi's looked like, but I'm sure it wasn't pretty. When I looked at it, however, it didn't occur to me that I might not have done a perfect mending job. I only felt pride that I had done it.

As for my mom, I have wondered what she felt when she saw me walk out the door to school wearing those patched-knee trousers. Some mothers might have been embarrassed to have their child seen in such tatters—that it evidenced how few pennies our family had to spare. But I think my mom didn't even look at my Levi's. I think she was looking at me, and probably saw in me the same thing I saw in the patch:

"I did that."

## Children Learn When They Are Ready to Learn

Denying children the opportunity to develop their processes is not the only way outsourcing has damaged their capabilities, either. There is something far more important at risk when we outsource too much of our lives: our values.

Not long ago, I was complimenting a friend on how his children had turned into such terrific adults. He and his wife (I'll call them Jim and Norma) had raised a wonderful family. Each of their five children turned out to be *very* different from one another. But all of them were successful in their careers, had chosen wonderful spouses, and were now raising children of their own, each in different parts of the country.

I asked Jim and Norma about how they had raised such great children. Of all the gems of wisdom that they shared with me, this insight, from Norma, stood out: "When the kids come home for a family reunion, I like to listen to their banter back and forth about the experiences they had growing up, and which had the greatest impact on their lives. I typically have no memory of the events they recall as being important. And when I ask them about the times when Jim and I sat them down specifically to share what we thought were foundationally important values of our family, well, the kids have no memory of any of them. I guess the thing to learn from this is that children will learn when they are ready to learn, not when we're ready to teach them."

It's a beautiful way of articulating the importance of building the third of the capabilities—priorities. It affects what our children will put first in their lives. In fact, it may be the single most important capability we can give our kids.

You can probably recall similar moments from your own childhood—the times that you picked up something important from your parents that they probably weren't aware they were sharing. Your parents most likely weren't thinking consciously about teaching you the right priorities at the time—but simply because they were there with you in those learning moments, those values became your values, too. Which means that first, when children are ready to learn, we need to be there. And second, we need to be found displaying through our actions, the priorities and values that we want our children to learn.

Yet again, in outsourcing much of the work that formerly

filled our homes, we have created a void in our children's lives that often gets filled with activities in which we are not involved. And as a result, when our children are ready to learn, it is often people whom we do not know or respect who are going to be there.

There's a wonderful conundrum left to us by the Greeks. It was first put to print by the author Plutarch, and it's known as the Ship of Theseus. As a tribute to the mythical founder of their city—famed for slaying the Minotaur—the Athenians committed to keeping Theseus's ship seaworthy in the harbor of Athens. As parts of the boat decayed, they were replaced . . . until eventually, every last part of the boat had been changed.

The conundrum was this: given that every last part of it had been replaced, was it still Theseus's ship? The Athenians still called it Theseus's Ship . . . but was it?

I want to turn that into a similar philosophical question for you: if your children gain their priorities and values from other people . . . whose children are they?

Yes, they are still your children—but you see what I'm getting at. The risk is not that every moment spent with another adult will be indelibly transferring inferior values. Nor is this about making the argument that you need to protect your children from the "big bad world"—that you must spend every waking moment with them. You shouldn't. Balance is important, and there are valuable lessons your children will gain from facing the challenges that life will throw at them on their own.

Rather, the point is that even if you're doing it with the best of intentions, if you find yourself heading down a path of outsourcing more and more of your role as a parent, you will lose more and more of the precious opportunities to help your kids develop their values—which may be the most important capability of all.

~

*You have your children's best interests at heart when you provide them with resources. It's what most parents think they're supposed to do—provide for their child. You can compare with your neighbors and friends how many activities your child is involved in, what instruments he is learning, what sports she is playing. It's easy to measure and it makes you feel good. But too much of this loving gesture can actually undermine their becoming the adults you want them to be.*

*Children need to do more than learn new skills. The theory of* capabilities *suggests they need to be challenged. They need to solve hard problems. They need to develop values. When you find yourself providing more and more experiences that are not giving children an opportunity to be deeply engaged, you are not equipping them with the processes they need to succeed in the future. And if you find yourself handing your children over to other people to give them all these experiences—outsourcing—you are, in fact, losing valuable opportunities to help nurture and develop them into the kind of adults you respect and admire. Children will learn when they're ready to learn, not when you're ready to teach them; if you are not with them as they encounter challenges in their lives, then you are missing important opportunities to shape their priorities—and their lives.*

# CHAPTER EIGHT

# The Schools of Experience

*Helping your children learn how to do difficult things is one of the most important roles of a parent. It will be critical to equipping them for all the challenges that life will throw at them down the line. But how do you equip your kids with the* right *capabilities?*

~

## Is It Really the Right Stuff?

In 1979, writer Tom Wolfe captured the public imagination with his depiction of one of the most competitive professional environments in the world: the screening of American fighter pilots. To find out who should rise to the top, the pilots battled it out in an ever-increasing test of nerves, a kind of Darwinian gauntlet. Early NASA executives had decided this was how to identify who had been born with the "right stuff." Those who thrived under the white-knuckle pressure of the program were deemed natural-born heroes.

Many companies looking to make top staffing decisions tend to replicate the same kind of thinking: that somehow there is a definitive way to identify the difference between the good and the great. In business, the "test" is what a résumé shows; you can tell by this whether a candidate is likely to thrive in a challenging new position. Underlying this is a belief that top candidates achieved what they did because of innate talent; that all these talents were qualities the candidate was born with, lying dormant, waiting to be used and honed. Recruiters search for those candidates who have gone from success to success to success, a kind of business version of the fighter-pilot tests. On paper, top candidates always seem to stand out. They have Wolfe's term, "the right stuff."

But if a candidate ever moved horizontally or had assignments that weren't clear promotions, a lot of recruiters assume that person lacks the "right stuff"; it's as if their company has indicated that they have reached the limits of their talent.

If finding the right stuff is a good way to identify top talent, why is it so common to see executives with a successful track record in one company coming into another company with great fanfare—only to be quickly dubbed a failure and ushered out? There is clearly something wrong here. The idea that some people have innate talents that just need to be identified has proved to be an unreliable predictor of success in business. Companies are using what would seem to be a logical list of criteria to screen their top candidates, but it's the wrong list.

Several years ago, in a major executive education program for over a thousand senior leaders from a variety of companies, I asked by survey this question: "Of all of the people that you hired or promoted into positions of (defined) responsibility in your company since you've had your current responsibility, what percentage of them turned out to be a superb choice? What percentage is performing adequately? And what percentage turned out to have been the wrong person for the job they were hired or promoted to do?" By their own reckoning, about a third were superb choices; 40 percent were adequate choices; and about 25 percent turned out to be mistakes.

In other words, a typical manager gets it wrong *a lot*. They may strive for zero-defect quality in manufacturing or services, but a 25-percent "defect" rate in picking the right people—what many consider their most important responsibility—is somehow considered acceptable.

So if a "right stuff" screen doesn't predict future success, what does? I spent a lot of time searching for and attempting to develop a theory that would help my students avoid such hiring mistakes in their future careers. In my hunt, I read book after book where the thinking had been reduced to generalities. They all wrote about the need to get "the right people in the right spots at the right time" and took examples of successful companies as the basis for "rules" of how to do this. Most of the books I read assumed the choices that one successful company had made would work for everyone. "If you hire the types of people that successful company XYZ Inc. did—then you will be successful, too."

That's a bad way to develop theory. In fact, it's not theory at all. Most of these conclusions are based on anecdotes and hearsay.

It wasn't until I came across work initially developed by Morgan McCall, a professor at the University of Southern California, in a book called *High Flyers*, that I finally found a theory that could help people make better decisions about whom to hire in their future. It explained why so many managers make hiring mistakes.

McCall has a very different view of the "right stuff." While Wolfe's fighter pilots may indeed have been the best of the best, McCall's theory gives a causal explanation of why. It wasn't because they were born with superior skills. Instead, it was because they had honed them along the way, by having experiences that taught them how to deal with setbacks or extreme stress in high-stakes situations.

The "right stuff" thinking lists skills that are *correlated* with success. It is, using the description of theory discussed earlier, looking to see whether job candidates have wings and feathers. McCall's schools of experience model asks whether they have actually flown, and if so, in what circumstances. This model helps identify whether, in an earlier assignment, someone has actually wrestled with a problem similar to the one he will need to wrestle with now. In terms of the language of the capabilities from earlier, it is a search for process capabilities.

Unlike the "right stuff" model, McCall's thinking is not based on the idea that great leaders are born ready to go. Rather, their abilities are developed and shaped by experiences in life. A challenging job, a failure in leading a project, an assignment in a new area of the company—all those things become "courses" in the school of experience. The skills that leaders have—or lack—depend heavily on which "courses," so to speak, they have and have not taken along the way.

## The Right Stuff Isn't Right at All

I have made mistakes with assessing managers over the years more frequently than I care to admit by not using McCall's thinking. For example, I fell short when I was running CPS Technologies, which made products out of a class of high-technology ceramics materials like aluminum oxide and silicon nitride. Two years into our start-up, we were ready to move into low-level manufacturing of our initial products, and we decided that we needed to hire a vice president of operations. Neither I nor my MIT-professor colleagues had ever scaled-up a manufacturing process before. The VP's immediate responsibility was going to be to do this—to grow our operations out of the lab and into production in our new plant, which was about five miles away from our laboratories.

After three months of searching, we had narrowed the search down to two people. A venture capitalist on our board referred Candidate A to us—a *very* capable man, who was executive vice president of operations for a multibillion-dollar business unit that spanned the globe. We admired the quality of their products, which included very sophisticated zirconium oxide products that could withstand fast swings in temperature without fracturing. Our second option, Candidate B, had been the boss of Rick, one of our most respected engineers. Rick highly recommended him. Candidate B had been on the front lines of his company, and it showed: the guy literally had dirt under his fingernails. He had just shut down two plants, which made traditional-technology ceramics products like aluminum oxide in electric insulation applications, near Erie, Pennsylvania, to get out of costly union contracts. He had transported much of their process equipment to a rural town in Tennessee, where they had opened a new plant just three months earlier. He did not have a college degree.

The senior managers in our company were leaning toward the guy with the dirty fingernails. But the two venture capital investors on the board were strongly in favor of Candidate A. They had very high hopes for CPS Technologies, and Candidate A was a senior executive in a company that we wanted to grow to emulate. He knew from the inside out how a global company operated at the high-technology end of the materials spectrum. Candidate A was responsible for nearly $2 billion in sales globally. Our VCs disparaged Candidate B because of his low-technology background. Candidate B's company was family-owned, and typically generated $30 million in revenues.

In the end, we decided on Candidate A, and spent about $250,000 helping him relocate from Tokyo to Boston. He was a nice man, but he badly managed the ramp-up of the process and the plant. We had to ask him to resign within eighteen months. By that time, Candidate B had taken another job, so we had to initiate yet another search.

At the time, we didn't have McCall's theory to guide us—but I sure wish we had. Candidate A had presided over a massive operation, but one that was in a steady state. He had never started and built anything before—and as a consequence, he knew nothing of the problems that one encounters when starting up a new factory and scaling production of a new process. Furthermore, because of the scale of his operation, Candidate A had a large group of direct reports. He managed through them, rather than working shoulder by shoulder with them.

When we compared the candidates' résumés, Candidate A won hands-down. He had the "right stuff"—the *adjectives* about him just blew Candidate B out of the water. But that didn't make him right for us. Had we looked for the *past-tense verbs* on their résumés, however, Candidate B would have won hands-down—because the résumé would have shown that he had taken the right courses in the schools of experience—including a field graduate seminar called "Scaling up process technology from the lab, through pilot scale, and then full scale." He had wrestled with problems that the rest of us did not even know we were going to face.

Or, in other words, he had the right processes to do the job. In expressing a preference for the more polished candidate, we biased ourselves toward resources over the processes. It is what I described in the previous chapter as something parents do, and it's an easy mistake to make. Even big companies get this wrong all the time. Take, for example, the story of Pandesic, an extraordinary collaboration between two of the world's technology giants, Intel and SAP. They made exactly the same mistake that my colleagues and I made in hiring the wrong VP-Operations at CPS Technologies—just on a much larger scale.

Pandesic was designed to create a more affordable version of SAP's enterprise resource-planning software, targeted at small and midsize companies. It was founded in 1997 with high hopes—and $100 million in funding. Intel and SAP both handpicked some of their most highly regarded people to lead this prominent joint venture.

But just three years later, it was declared a colossal failure. Virtually nothing had worked out as planned.

While it's always easy to play Monday-morning quarterback about everything that should have been done differently, one thing *is* clear in hindsight: though the people picked by those companies to run the project were highly experienced, they were not the right people for the job.

Through the lens of McCall's theory, it begins to make sense why. While Pandesic's senior management team had stellar résumés, not one of them had experience launching a new venture. None of them knew how to adjust a strategy when the first one didn't work. None had had to figure out how to make a brand-new product profitable before growing it big.

The Pandesic team had been used to running orderly, well-resourced initiatives for their respective world-class companies. What Intel and SAP had done was handpick a team that could run an equivalent of either of the giants, but not a start-up. The team members hadn't been to the right school to create and drive a new-growth project. That relegated Pandesic to a footnote in Intel's and SAP's histories.

## Planning Your Courses at the Schools of Experience

If you think about McCall's theory, going through the right courses in the schools of experience can help people in all kinds of situations increase the likelihood of success.

One of the CEOs I have most admired, Nolan Archibald, has spoken to my students on this theory. Archibald has had a stellar career, including having been the youngest-ever CEO of a Fortune 500 company—Black & Decker.

After he retired, he discussed with my students how he'd managed his career. What he described was not all of the steps on his résumé, but rather *why* he took them. Though he didn't use this language, he built his career by registering for specific courses in the schools of experience. Archibald had a clear goal in mind when he graduated from college— he wanted to become CEO of a successful company. But instead of setting out on what most people thought would be the "right," prestigious stepping-stone jobs to get there, he asked himself: "What are all the experiences and problems that I have to learn about and master so that what comes out at the other end is somebody who is ready and capable of becoming a successful CEO?"

That meant Archibald was prepared to make some unconventional moves in the early years of his career—moves his peers at business school might not have understood on the surface. Instead of taking jobs or assignments because they looked like a fast-track to the C-suite, he chose his options very deliberately for the experience they would provide. "I wouldn't ever make the decision based upon how much it paid or the prestige," he told my students "Instead, it was always: is it going to give me the experiences I need to wrestle with?"

His first job after business school was not a glamorous consulting position. Instead, he worked in Northern Quebec, operating an asbestos mine. He thought that particular experience, of managing and leading people in difficult conditions, would be important to have mastered on his route to the C-suite. It was the first of many such decisions he made.

The strategy worked. It wasn't long before he became CEO of Beatrice Foods. And then, at age forty-two, he achieved an even loftier goal: he was appointed CEO of Black & Decker. He stayed in that position for twenty-four years.

## A Course for Just Five Players

Does that mean that we should never hire or promote an inexperienced manager who had not already learned to do what needs to be done in this assignment? The answer: it depends. In a start-up company where there are no processes in place to get things done, then everything that is done must be done by individual people—resources. In this circumstance, it would be risky to draft someone with no experience to do the job—because in the absence of processes that can guide people, experienced people need to lead. But in established companies where much of the guidance to employees is provided by processes, and is less dependent upon managers with detailed, hands-on experience, then it makes sense to hire or promote someone who needs to learn from experience.

The value of giving people experiences before they need them plays out in many fields other than business. The coach of one of my favorite basketball teams while I was growing up was always just *driven* to win and to win big. As one of his biggest fans, I loved watching my team blowing out its competitors by margins of thirty points. I always knew the names of the five starting players. I generally knew the names of one or two of the "bench" players, too—because they occasionally logged minutes in the game. But the other players further down the bench were anonymous to me—because the coach kept playing the five best players right down to the end when he was confident that no one could blow the wide lead. This often meant that we won by thirty-five rather than twenty-five points—and as a young boy who worshipped this team, I could not have asked for more.

The players further down the bench did occasionally log "garbage time"—one or two minutes at the end when it didn't matter what anybody did. My friends and I referred to them as "scrubs." Somehow I missed the fact that these were brilliant players on one of the best teams in the world—so good that tens of thousands of other really good players had failed to make a slot on that team.

I remember, however, a particular game when I real-ized the limitations to the coach's drive to always win big. As usual, they'd made it all the way to the championship game. But this year, the team they were competing against was play-ing particularly well. Our starting team had to work harder than ever to try to get the lead the coach expected. By the end of the third quarter, the starters were exhausted. I remember watching the coach on TV. He looked all the way down to the end of the bench. He never bothered to do that in typical matches until the final few minutes of the game, when the stakes were no longer high. This time, however, he needed someone to put into the game at that critical moment. But there was a problem: he didn't see anyone on the bench whom he trusted—because he had never before put them into tight situations where they could have honed their abilities to per-form under pressure. So he had to keep playing his weary starters. They lost that game—and the league championship.

The coach's school of experience didn't offer open en-rollment in a course on "How to deal with pressure." It was closed for everyone except his five starting players. And the team paid the price.

## Sending Your Kids to the Right School

Thinking back on your own life, I bet you had many visits to various schools of experience, some—like the basketball team's course on dealing with pressure—more painful than others. Obviously, it will help a lot if you can work out which courses will be important for you to master *before* you need them.

As a parent, you can find small opportunities for your child to take important courses early on. You're doing what Nolan Archibald did, working out what courses your child will need to be successful and then reverse engineering the right experiences. Encourage them to stretch—to aim for lofty goals. If they don't succeed, make sure you're there to help them learn the right lesson: that when you aim to achieve great things, it is inevitable that sometimes you're not going to make it. Urge them to pick themselves up, dust themselves off, and try again. Tell them that if they're not occasionally failing, then they're not aiming high enough. Everyone knows how to celebrate success, but you should also celebrate failure if it's as a result of a child striving for an out-of-reach goal.

This can be difficult for parents to do. So much of our society's culture is focused on trying to build self-esteem in children by never letting them lose a game, giving them accolades simply for trying their best, and constantly receiving feedback from teachers or coaches that never requires them to think about whether they can do better. From a very young age, many of our children who participate in sports come to expect medals, trophies, or ribbons at the end of a season—simply for participating. Those medals and awards end up in a pile in a corner of their bedroom over the years and quickly become meaningless to those kids. They haven't really learned anything from them.

In some ways, the awards are really for the parents—it is often we who get the most out of seeing the accumulation of medals and ribbons. It sure feels better to congratulate our kids on their achievements than it does to console them for a tough failure. In fact, it's very tempting for many parents to step in to ensure that their child is always succeeding. But what are they getting from that?

When I worked with Boy Scouts over the years, I always wanted the kids to take responsibility for organizing their own camping trips rather than letting the parents step in to do it. When they had to do it themselves, they learned how to plan and organize, how to divide responsibilities, how to communicate among a group, and to appreciate what they'd actually put their own work into.

It sure would have been easier to allow the parents to work through and divide up the tasks on the "to do" list for every trip. We probably would have prepared efficiently for every eventuality—and the boys would certainly have had fun. All they would have had to do was show up. But we would have been denying them important courses—leadership, organization, and accountability.

We have many opportunities to help our children take courses in life—and not all of them are good. Many parents, for example, find themselves in a situation that probably happens at dinner tables all over the world: a child announces that he has a big report or project due the next day and he hasn't started it. The grade on that report does matter and no one wants to see his child get poor marks. Panic ensues.

What should a parent do?

Not only will many parents stay up late to help their child complete the project, some parents might even finish it for him, hoping it helps their child get a good grade. All kinds of good intentions are at work: they may hope that the good grade will help the child maintain a healthy self-esteem. They might even think, "If I step in to finish this for my child, at least he will get a good night's sleep to help him face tomorrow's challenges in school. I've helped my child through this rough spot. I'm being a supportive parent."

But think about what course you have just given your child with the decision to bail him out. You've given him the Cliffs Notes course; you've taken him through the experience of learning how to take shortcuts. He'll think, My parents will be there to solve hard problems for me. I won't have to figure it out on my own. Good grades are what matters, much more than doing the work.

What do you think will happen next time your child is late on a project? He'll announce at the dinner table that he needs help. And you will find yourself, again, finishing it up for him at three a.m.

The braver decision for parents may be to give that child a more difficult, but also more valuable, course in life. Allow the child to see the consequences of neglecting an important assignment. Either he will have to stay up late on his own to pull it off, or he will see what happens when he fails to complete it. And yes, that child might get a bad grade. That might be even more painful for the parent to witness than the child. But that child will likely not feel good about what he allowed to happen, which is the first lesson in the course on taking responsibility for yourself.

## Engineering Courses

Our default instincts are so often just to support our children in a difficult moment. But if our children don't face difficult challenges, and sometimes fail along the way, they will not build the resilience they will need throughout their lives. People who hit their first significant career roadblock after years of nonstop achievement often fall apart.

As a parent, you don't want that to happen to your own child. You should consciously think about what abilities you want your child to develop, and then what experiences will likely help him get them. So you might have to think about engineering opportunities for your child to have the experiences you believe will help him develop the capabilities he needs for life. That may not be easy, but it will be worthwhile.

One friend of mine recently noticed that her eight-year-old daughter had more or less plagiarized the dust jacket for a school book report. She spoke to her daughter gently about thinking those words weren't her own. "What does 'come to terms with the father who abandoned him' mean?" she challenged her daughter. But her daughter didn't respond well. "It's fine, Mom. It doesn't matter."

Now, this mom knew that plagiarism is a big deal. It can derail a promising high school or college career, never mind completely ruin a professional one. So she decided to ask the teacher to help her create an experience for her child. Together they engineered a moment that would privately, gently embarrass her daughter when the teacher recognized what she had done. Whatever the teacher said, it worked. When her daughter came home from school that day, she simply went to the computer to "edit" her report—and what emerged were entirely her own words. Not so beautifully written or thoughtful, but they were her own. My friend had given her daughter a valuable experience when the stakes were not yet high, hoping that prevents the same thing from recurring later when it would likely matter much more.

Creating experiences for your children doesn't guarantee that they'll learn what they need to learn. If that doesn't happen, you have to figure out why that experience didn't achieve it. You might have to iterate through different ideas until you get it right. The important thing for a parent is, as always, to never give up; never stop trying to help your children get the right experiences to prepare them for life.

Like in the example with our hiring managers at the start of this chapter, it's tempting to judge success by a résumé— by looking at the scoreboard of what our children have achieved. But much more important in the long run is what courses our kids have taken as they've gone through the various schools of experience. More than any award or trophy, this is the best way to equip them for success as they venture out into the world.

~

*The challenges your children face serve an important purpose: they will help them hone and develop the capabilities necessary to succeed throughout their lives. Coping with a difficult teacher, failing at a sport, learning to navigate the complex social structure of cliques in school—all those things become "courses" in* the *school of experience. We know that people who fail in their jobs often do so not because they are inherently incapable of succeeding, but because their experiences have not prepared them for the challenges of that job—in other words, they've taken the wrong "courses."*

*The natural tendency of many parents is to focus entirely on building your child's résumé: good grades, sports successes, and so on. It would be a mistake, however, to neglect the courses your children need to equip them for the future. Once you have that figured out, work backward: find the right experiences to help them build the skills they'll need to succeed. It's one of the greatest gifts you can give them.*

# CHAPTER NINE

# The Invisible Hand Inside Your Family

*Most of us have—or had—an idyllic image of what our families would be like. The children will be well-behaved, they'll adore and respect us, we'll enjoy spending time together, and they'll make us proud when they are off in the world without us by their side.*

*And yet, as any experienced parent will tell you, wishing for that kind of family and actually having that kind of family are two very different things. One of the most powerful tools to enable us to close the gap between the family we want and the family we get is culture. We need to understand how it works and be prepared to put in the hard yards to influence how it is shaped.*

~

## When the Chariot Goes Over the Hill

As parents, we share a common worry: one day, our children are going to be faced with a tough decision . . . and we are not going to be there to make sure they do the right thing. They're going to get on a plane and fly to a far-flung country with their friends. Or get to college and see a chance to cheat on a test. Perhaps they'll face a decision whether to choose to be kind to a complete stranger—to do something that will make a huge difference in that person's life. All we can do is hope that somehow we've raised them well enough that they come to the right conclusion by themselves.

But here's the question: how do we make sure that happens?

It's not as simple as setting family rules and hoping for the best. Something more fundamental has to occur—and it has to happen years before the moment arises when our children are faced with that difficult choice. Their priorities need to be set correctly so they will know how to evaluate their options and make a good choice. The best tool we have to help our children do this is through the culture we build in our families.

Enterprises and families are very similar in this respect. Just like your parents wanted you to make good decisions, business leaders want to ensure that midlevel managers and employees everywhere in the company make the right choices every day without requiring constant supervision. This is nothing new: as far back as ancient Rome, emperors would send an associate off to govern a newly conquered territory thousands of miles away. As the emperors watched the chariot go over the hill—knowing full well they would not see their associate again for years—they needed to know that their understudy's priorities were consistent with their own, and that he would use proven, accepted methods to solve problems. Culture was the only way to make sure this happened.

## How Does Culture Form in a Company?

Culture. It is a word we hear so much of on a day-to-day basis, and many of us associate it with different things. In the case of a company, it's common to describe culture as the visible elements of a working environment: casual Fridays, free sodas in the cafeteria, or whether you can bring your dog into the office. But as MIT's Edgar Schein—one of the world's leading scholars on organizational culture—explains, those things don't define a culture. They're just artifacts of it. An office that allows T-shirts and shorts could also be a very hierarchical place. Would that still be a "casual" culture?

Culture is far more than general office tone or guidelines. Schein defined culture, and how it is formed, in these terms:

> Culture is a way of working together toward common goals that have been followed so frequently and so successfully that people don't even think about trying to do things another way. If a culture has formed, people will autonomously do what they need to do to be successful.

Those instincts aren't formed overnight. Rather, they are the result of shared learning—of employees working together to solve problems and figuring out what works. In every organization, there is that first time when a problem or challenge arises. "How do we deal with this customer's complaint?" "Should we delay introducing this product until we've been able to go through another round of quality testing?" "Which of our customers is the top priority?" "Whose demands will we pay attention to, whose can we ignore?" "Is 'good enough' an acceptable standard for deciding when a new product is ready to ship?"

In each instance of a problem or task arising, those responsible reached a decision together on what to do and how to do it in order to succeed. If that decision and its associated action resulted in a successful outcome—"good enough" product quality made the customer happy, for example— then the next time when those employees faced a similar type of challenge, they would return to the same decision and same way of solving the problem. If, on the other hand, it failed—the customer stormed off and the employees' manager reprimanded them—those employees would be extremely hesitant to take that approach again. Every time they tackle a problem, employees aren't just solving the problem itself; in solving it, they are learning what matters. In the language of capabilities from the previous chapters, they are creating an understanding of the priorities in the business, and how to execute them—the processes. A culture is the unique combination of processes and priorities within an organization.

As long as the way they have chosen keeps working to solve the problem—it doesn't have to be perfect, but working well enough—the culture will coalesce and become an internal set of rules and guidelines that employees in the company will draw upon in making the choices ahead of them. If these paradigms of how to work together, and of what things should be given priority over other things, are used successfully over and over again, ultimately employees won't stop and ask each other how they should work together. They will just *assume* that the way they have been doing it is *the way* of doing it. The advantage of this is that it effectively causes an organization to become self-managing. Managers don't need to be omnipresent to enforce the rules. People instinctively get on with what needs to be done.

There are many examples of firms with powerful cultures.

Pixar, for example, which is known for highly creative and critically acclaimed children's films such as *Finding Nemo*, *Up*, and *Toy Story*, might not seem that different from other animation studios on paper. But Pixar has developed a unique culture.

To begin with, its creative *process* is very different. Many film studios have a development department to come up with the ideas for movies, and then they hand those ideas out to directors to make a film. But Pixar does it differently. Instead of the group creating ideas and assigning them to directors to execute, Pixar recognizes that directors are naturally going to be more motivated to build out their own ideas—so it focuses on helping directors refine them. The Pixar development team provides daily input to build a story, and they do this for every film in progress across the company. That process includes no-holds-barred feedback from people who are not involved in the making of each film. They can be brutally honest sessions. Yet Pixar's employees have come to respect that honesty because everyone at Pixar agrees on the same goal: making high-quality, original films. That's the *priority*. Unvarnished feedback is valued because it helps to make better movies.

These processes and priorities have coalesced into Pixar's creative culture. Because working this way in film after film has been so successful, the culture has crystallized and now people don't feel they should hold back from criticizing a film's story because it might derail the timetable. They know it's more important to produce a great movie.

That's not to say that the way of working together at Pixar is the way that every company in the film industry should work. Rather, we can simply say that the folks at Pixar have used this way of working very successfully, year after year. Now the employees don't even need to ask how to behave, how to make decisions, or how to make this trade-off against that one. Pixar has become in many ways a self-managing company, thanks to its culture. Management doesn't need to dive into the details of every decision, because the culture— almost as an agent of management—is present in the details of every decision.

As long as the company's competitive and technological environments remain as they are today, the strength of its culture is a blessing. If the environment changes substantially, however, then the strength of the culture will make it hard to change things, too.

Schein's articulation of how culture is created allows executives to create a culture for their organization—provided that they follow the rules. It starts with defining a problem—one that recurs again and again. Next, they must ask a group to figure out how to solve that problem. If they fail, ask them to find a better way to solve it. Once they've succeeded, however, the managers need to ask the same team to solve the problem every time it recurs—over and over again. The more often they solve the problem successfully, the more instinctive it becomes to do it in the way that they designed. Culture in any organization is formed through repetition. That way of doing things becomes the group's culture.

Many companies see the value in assertively shaping their culture—so that the culture, rather than the managers, causes the right things to happen. Once it has been shown to work, they write it down and talk about it, as often as possible. Netflix, for example, invested a great deal of time in defining and writing down its culture—one that may not suit everybody. Not only is this available to employees, but it's freely available online. It includes:

- *No vacation policy: take as much as you want, as long as you're doing a great job and covering your responsibilities.*
- *"Outstanding" employees only: doing an "adequate" job*

leads to your getting a "generous severance package," so
the company can hire an A-player in your place.
- "Freedom and responsibility" vs. command-and-
control: good managers give their employees the right
context in which to make decisions—and then the
employees make the decisions.

But management can't just spend time communicating
what the culture is—it must make decisions that are entirely
in alignment with it. While Netflix built an early reputation
for doing this, it's not uncommon to see a company release a
document about culture, and then completely fail to live up
to it.

Famous examples abound—Enron had a "Vision and
Values" statement. It aimed to conduct itself in line with four
Values (each starting with a capital letter): Respect, Integrity,
Communication, and Excellence. Respect, for example, had
the following detail (as reported in the *New York Times*): "We
treat others as we would like to be treated ourselves. We do
not tolerate abusive or disrespectful treatment. Ruthlessness,
callousness, and arrogance don't belong here."

Clearly, all the way from the top, Enron did not live the
values it espoused. If you don't articulate a culture—or articulate one but don't enforce it—then a culture is still going
to emerge. However, it is going to be based on the processes
and priorities that have been repeated within the organization and have worked.

You can tell the health of a company's culture by asking, "When faced with a choice on how to do something, did employees make the decision that the culture 'wanted' them to make? And was the feedback they received consistent with that?" If these elements aren't actively managed, then a single wrong decision or wrong outcome can quite easily send a firm's culture down entirely the wrong path.

### This Is the Way Our Family Behaves

The parallels between a business and a family should be clear. Just like a manager who wants to count on employees using the right priorities to solve problems, parents want to set those priorities, too, so that family members will solve problems and confront dilemmas instinctively, whether or not the parents are there guiding or observing. Kids won't have to stop and think about what Mom or Dad wants them to do—they'll just go about it because their family culture has dictated, "This is the way our family behaves."

A culture can be built consciously or evolve inadvertently. If you want your family to have a culture with a clear set of priorities for everyone to follow, then those priorities need to be proactively designed into the culture—which can be built through the steps noted above. It needs to be shaped the way that you want it to be in your family, and you have to think about this early on. If you want your family to have a culture of kindness, then the first time one of your kids approaches a problem where kindness is an option—help him choose it, and then help him succeed through kindness. Or if he doesn't choose it, call him on it and explain why he should have chosen differently.

That's not to say that any of this is easy. First, you come into a family with a culture from the family in which you grew up. There's a good chance your spouse's family culture will have been fundamentally different from yours. Just getting the two of you to agree on anything is a miracle. Then add kids to the equation—they're born with their own attitudes and wiring. Yes, it's going to be difficult, but that's exactly why it's so important to understand what type of culture you want and to proactively pursue it.

My wife, Christine, and I started, when we were newly engaged, with an end goal—a specific family culture—in mind. We didn't think about it in terms of culture, but that's what we were doing. We decided in a deliberate fashion that we wanted our children to love each other and to support each other. We decided we wanted our children to have an instinct to obey God. We decided we wanted them to be kind. And, finally, we decided that we wanted them to love work.

The culture we picked is the right culture for our family, but every family should choose a culture that's right for them. What is important is to actively choose what matters to you, and then engineer the culture to reinforce those elements, as Schein's theory shows. It entails choosing what activities we pursue, and what outcomes we need to achieve, so that as a family, when we have to perform those activities again, we all think: "This is how we do it."

In our case, for example, we knew we couldn't simply

order our children to love work. Instead, we always tried to find ways for the kids to work together with us, and to make it fun. I would, for example, never work in the yard unless I had at least one—and often two—kids hanging on to the handle of the mower. For the longest time, they weren't really helping at all. Pushing a lawn mower with children hanging on, barely able to touch the ground, didn't make mowing easier. But that didn't matter. What really mattered was that it allowed us to define work for them as something that was a good thing. We did it together. It was fun, by definition. And I made sure that they knew they were helping Dad, helping the family.

Before long, this value became embedded in our family's culture; but it wasn't by magic or good luck. It was achieved by thoughtfully designing activities and doing simple things like mowing the lawn together. We tried to be consistent about it; we made sure the kids knew why we were doing it; and we always thanked them for it.

It is for this reason that as I look back at my life, I'm actually very glad we didn't have enough money to buy a perfectly finished house when our children were young. We stretched so far to buy that first wreck of a house that we later couldn't afford to pay tradesmen to fix it up for us. Everything that needed to be fixed had to be fixed by us and by the kids. Now, most people would think of this as a complete chore.

But inadvertently, we had moved our family into an environment rich in opportunities for us to work together. As tempting as it might otherwise have been, we couldn't outsource it—we simply could not afford to. This meant there wasn't a wall or a ceiling torn down, built up, plastered, or painted without the kids helping us to do it. We applied the same principles as with mowing the lawn—making it fun, and always thanking them. But in this instance, there was additional positive reinforcement: every time the kids walked into any room in the house, they'd see the wall and say: "I painted that wall." Or "I sanded it." Not only would they remember the fun we had in doing it together, but they felt the pride from seeing what they'd achieved. They learned to love work.

In solving the problems of fixing up our house together, we were helping to build the Christensen family culture. Doing things together, over and over, led to a mutual understanding of what things we prioritize, how we solve problems, and what really matters.

Make no mistake: a culture happens, whether you want it to or not. The only question is how hard you are going to try to influence it. Forming a culture is not an instant loop; it's not something you can decide on, communicate, and then expect it to suddenly work on its own. You need to be sure that when you ask your children to do something, or tell your spouse you're going to do something, you hold to that and follow through. It sounds obvious; most of us want to try to be consistent. But in the pressures of day-to-day living, that can be tough. There will be many days when enforcing the rules is harder on a parent than it is on a child. With good intentions, many exhausted parents find it too difficult to stay consistent with their rules early on—and inadvertently, they allow a culture of laziness or defiance to creep into their family.

Children might feel "success" in the short term by getting what they want in beating up a sibling, or talking back to a parent who finally relents to an unreasonable demand. Parents who let such behavior slide are essentially building a family culture—teaching their child that this is the way the world works, and that they can achieve their goals the same way each time.

You have to consciously work throughout the years your children are young to help them see "success" in the things you want to be part of your culture. For example, when one of our sons was very young, we learned that children in his class were bullying another child at school, and nobody was doing anything to stop it. Kindness had been one of our goals, but it had not yet become part of our culture. We came up with a new family motto: "We want Christensens to be known for kindness." We worked it into conversation—and, in particular, taught our son how he could help his classmate who had been bullied. We praised him when he helped his classmate, as well as any of our children when they demonstrated kindness to others. We made it part of our culture.

Over time, this had the effect we wanted. Each of our children became truly kind women and men. Wherever they are, in whatever corner of the world they are in, I do not worry about what they will do when confronted with a problem. The first thought in their minds will be "We want Christensens to be known for kindness."

Again, our choices for a family culture are not necessarily the right ones for everyone. What's important to understand is how culture is built, so that you have a chance to create the culture *you* want. In thinking about this, it might be helpful to remember the process by which strategy is defined. There are deliberate plans, and emergent problems and opportunities. These compete against one another in the resource allocation process, to determine which receive our highest priorities of time, energy, and talent. I observed that in my case, my profession emerged. My deliberate plan, to become editor of the *Wall Street Journal*, was swept to the side as other opportunities emerged—including my present profession as a teacher. However, I am grateful that I have not allowed the kind of person that I wanted to become to be left to chance. That was a very deliberate decision.

You should approach the creation of the culture for your family in similar terms. The professional pursuits and interests of your children need to emerge—and, in all probability, will be very different one from another. The culture of your family ought to welcome such diversity. But I recommend that, for the foundational dimensions of your family culture, there be uniformity. Getting this right will prove to be a source of happiness and pride for each of you.

Doing this does require constant vigilance about what is right and wrong. For every action a family member takes, imagine that it will happen all the time. Is that okay? Even something as simple as a fight between your two children that you didn't see. When one comes running to you in tears, how do you respond? Do you automatically punish the other child? Do you tell the crying child to shake it off? Do you call both of them together and punish both of them? Do you say you won't get involved? If whatever solution you choose seems to work, then each time that your kids run up against that same problem, they'll know what will happen. They will begin to learn the consequences of fighting with each other. If you are consistent, then even when they are playing at a friend's house, that's the behavior they will carry with them.

And if you don't? By the time many parents find themselves entering middle age with teenage children, they realize that they've allowed one of their most important jobs to slip past them. Left unchecked long enough, "once or twice" quickly becomes the culture. As these sets of behavior embed themselves in a family culture, they become very hard to change.

~

*All parents aspire to raise the kind of children that they know will make the right choices—even when they themselves are not there to supervise. One of the most effective ways to do that is to build the right family culture. It becomes the informal but powerful set of guidelines about how your family behaves.*

*As people work together to solve challenges repeatedly, norms begin to form. The same is true in your family: when you first run up against a problem or need to get something done together, you'll need to find a solution.*

*It's not just about controlling bad behavior; it's about celebrating the good. What does your family value? Is it creativity? Hard work? Entrepreneurship? Generosity? Humility? What do the kids know they have to do that will get their parents to say, "Well done"?*

*This is what is so powerful about culture. It's like an autopilot. What is critical to understand is that for it to be an effective force, you have to properly program the autopilot—you have to build the culture that you want in your family. If you do not consciously build it and reinforce it from the earliest stages of your family life, a culture will still form—but it will form in ways you may not like. Allowing your children to get away with lazy or disrespectful behavior a few times will begin the process of making it your family's culture. So will telling them that you're proud of them when they work hard to solve a problem. Although it's difficult for a parent to always be consistent and remember to give your children positive feedback when they do something right, it's in these everyday interactions that your culture is being set. And once that happens, it's almost impossible to change.*

# SECTION III

~

## *Staying Out of Jail*

The safest road to Hell is the gradual one—the gentle slope, soft underfoot, without sudden turnings, without milestones, without signposts.

—*C. S. Lewis*

U NTIL THIS POINT in the book, I've offered you a number of theories to help address the challenges you'll face in seeking happiness in your career and your life.

But in the final section of the book, I only want to use one theory to talk about living a life of integrity. In many respects, it is that simple. This section is intentionally short, but I believe it's equally powerful and universally applicable.

I can't anticipate all the circumstances and moral dilemmas you will find yourself in throughout your life. Yours will be different from everyone else's. What I offer here is a theory called "full versus marginal thinking" that will help you answer our final question: how can I be sure I live a life of integrity?

# CHAPTER TEN

## Just This Once . . .

*Most of us think that the important ethical decisions in our lives will be delivered with a blinking red neon sign:* CAUTION: IMPORTANT DECISION AHEAD. *Never mind how busy we are or what the consequences might be. Almost everyone is confident that in those moments of truth, he or she will do the right thing. After all, how many people do you know who believe they do not have integrity?*

*The problem is, life seldom works that way. It comes with no warning signs. Instead, most of us will face a series of small, everyday decisions that rarely seem like they have high stakes attached. But over time, they can play out far more dramatically.*

*It happens exactly the same way in companies. No company deliberately sets out to let itself be overtaken by its competitors. Rather, they are seemingly innocuous decisions that were made years before that led them down that path. This chapter will explain how that process happens so you can avoid falling into the most beguiling trap of all.*

~

## The Trap of Marginal Thinking

In the United States, in the late 1990s, Blockbuster dominated the movie rental industry. It had stores all over the country, a significant size advantage, and what appeared to be a stranglehold on the market. Blockbuster had made huge investments in its inventory for all its stores. But, obviously, it didn't make money from movies sitting on the shelves; it was only when a customer rented a movie, and a clerk scanned the movie out of the store, that Blockbuster made anything. It therefore needed to get the customer to watch the movie quickly, and then return it quickly, so that the clerk could rent the same DVD to different customers again and again. To prod customers to return the DVDs quickly, the company levied big fines for every day that the customer forgot to return the DVD on time—if Blockbuster didn't, it wouldn't make money, because the DVD would be sitting in a customer's home rather than be rented to someone else. It didn't take long before Blockbuster realized that people didn't like returning movies, so it increased late fees so much that analysts estimated that 70 percent of Blockbuster's profits were from these fees.

Set against this backdrop, a little upstart called Netflix emerged in the 1990s with a novel idea: rather than make people go to the video store, why don't we mail DVDs to them? Netflix's business model made profit in just the opposite way to Blockbuster's. Netflix customers paid a monthly fee—and the company made money when customers *didn't* watch the DVDs that they had ordered. As long as the DVDs sat unwatched at customers' homes, Netflix did not have to pay return postage—or send out the next batch of movies that the customer had already paid the monthly fee to get.

It was a bold move: Netflix was the quintessential David going up against the Goliath of the movie rental industry. Blockbuster had billions of dollars in assets, tens of thousands of employees, and 100 percent brand recognition. If Blockbuster decided it wanted to go after this nascent market, it would have the resources to make life very difficult for the little start-up.

But it didn't.

By 2002, the upstart was showing signs of potential. It had $150 million in revenues and a 36 percent profit margin. Blockbuster investors were starting to get nervous—there was clearly something to what Netflix was doing. Many pressured the incumbent to look more closely at the market.

So Blockbuster did. When it compared Netflix's numbers to its own, Blockbuster's management concluded, "Why would we bother?" The market Netflix was pursuing was smaller; it might get bigger, but it was unclear how big it had the potential to be. More troubling for Blockbuster's management, though, was that Netflix's profit margins were substantially smaller than what Blockbuster was used to. And if Blockbuster did decide to attack Netflix, and if it were successful, those efforts would most likely cannibalize sales from Blockbuster's very profitable stores. "Obviously, we pay attention to any way people are getting home entertainment. We always look at all those things," is how a Blockbuster's spokesperson responded to these concerns in a 2002 press release. "We have not seen a business model that is financially viable in the long term in this arena. Online rental services are 'serving a niche market.'"

Netflix, on the other hand, thought this market was fantastic. It didn't need to compare it to an existing and profitable business: its baseline was no profit and no business at all. Compared to that, Netflix was very happy with their relatively low margins and their "niche market."

So, who was right?

By 2011, Netflix had almost 24 million customers. And Blockbuster? It had declared bankruptcy the year before.

Blockbuster followed a principle that is taught in every fundamental course in finance and economics: that in evaluating alternative investments, we should ignore sunk and fixed costs (costs that have already been incurred), and instead base decisions on the marginal costs and marginal revenues (the new costs and revenues) that each alternative entails.

But it's a dangerous way of thinking. Almost always, such analysis shows that the marginal costs are lower, and marginal profits are higher, than the full cost. This doctrine biases companies to leverage what they have put in place to succeed in the past, instead of guiding them to create the capabilities they'll need in the future. If we knew the future would be exactly the same as the past, that approach would be fine. But if the future's different—and it almost always is—then it's the wrong thing to do.

Blockbuster looked at the DVD postal business using a marginal lens: it could only see it from the vantage point of its own existing business. When viewed like this, the market Netflix was going after did not look at all attractive. Worse, if Blockbuster did go after Netflix successfully, this new business was likely to kill Blockbuster's existing business. No CEO wants to tell shareholders that he wants to invest to create a new business that's going to be responsible for killing the existing business, especially if it's much less profitable. Who would go for that?

Netflix, on the other hand, had none of those concerns. There was nothing weighing it down—no marginal thinking. It assessed the opportunity using a completely clean sheet of paper. It didn't have to worry about maintaining existing stores or propping up existing margins; it didn't have any. All Netflix saw was a huge opportunity . . . the exact same opportunity that Blockbuster should have seen, but couldn't.

Marginal thinking made Blockbuster believe that the alternative to not pursuing the postal DVD market was to happily continue doing what it was doing before, at 66 percent margins and billions of dollars in revenue. But the real alternative to not going after Netflix was, in fact, bankruptcy. The right way to look at this new market was not to think, "How can we protect our existing business?" Instead, Blockbuster should have been thinking: "If we didn't have an existing business, how could we best build a new one? What would be the best way for us to serve our customers?" Blockbuster couldn't bring itself to do it, so Netflix did instead. And when Blockbuster declared bankruptcy in 2010, the existing business that it had been so eager to preserve by using a marginal strategy was lost anyway.

This is almost always how it plays out. Because failure is often at the end of a path of marginal thinking, we end up paying for the full cost of our decisions, not the marginal costs, whether we like it or not.

### You End Up Paying the Full Price Anyway

Another one of the most famous examples of the destructive power of marginal thinking is the steel industry. U.S. Steel, one of the world's foremost traditional steel manufacturers, had been watching its competitor, Nucor Steel, find new lower-level markets in the steel industry. Nucor had succeeded in getting an edge in this market by using lower-cost technology than the traditional makers had for making steel, in new types of plants called "mini-mills."

As Nucor began to eat into U.S. Steel's market, a group of engineers at U.S. Steel got together and concluded that if U.S. Steel was going to survive, it had to build the kind of steel mills that Nucor had. That way, it could create steel products at a much lower cost, remaining competitive against Nucor. So the engineers put together a business plan, which showed that U.S. Steel's profit per ton would increase sixfold in the new plant.

Everybody agreed this was a promising plan . . . everybody except the chief financial officer. When he saw that the plan involved spending money to build new mills, he put the brakes on. "Why should we build a new mill? We have 30 percent excess capacity in our existing mills. If you want to sell an extra ton of steel, make it in our existing mills. The marginal cost of producing an additional ton in our existing mills is so low that the marginal profit is four times greater than if we build a completely new mini-mill."

The CFO made the marginal-thinking mistake. He didn't see that by utilizing the existing plant, they were not changing their fundamental cost of making steel at all. Building a completely new mill would have had an up-front cost, but then given the company a new and important capability for the future.

These case studies helped me resolve a paradox that has appeared repeatedly in my attempts to help established companies that are confronted by disruptive entrants—as was the case with Blockbuster and U.S. Steel. Once their executives understood the peril that the disruptive attackers posed, I would say, "Okay. Now the problem is that your sales force is not going to be able to sell these disruptive products. They need to be sold to different customers, for different purposes. You need to create a different sales force."

Inevitably they would respond, "Clay, you're just naive. You have no idea how much it costs to create a new sales force. We need to leverage our existing sales team."

Or I would say, "You know that brand of yours? It isn't going to work on this new disruptive product. You need to build a different brand."

Their response was just the same. "Clay, you have no idea how expensive it is to create a new brand from scratch. We need to leverage one of our existing brands."

The language of the disruptive attackers was completely different: "It's time to create the sales force" and "It's time to build a brand."

Hence, the paradox: Why is it that the big, established companies that have so much capital find these initiatives to be so costly? And why do the small entrants with much less capital find them to be straightforward?

The answer is in the theory of marginal versus full costs. Every time an executive in an established company needs to make an investment decision, there are two alternatives on the menu. The first is the full cost of making something completely new. The second is to leverage what already exists, so that you only need to incur the marginal cost and revenue. Almost always, the marginal-cost argument overwhelms the full-cost. For the entrant, in contrast, there is no marginal-cost item on the menu. If it makes sense, then you do the full-cost alternative. Because they are new to the scene, in fact, the full cost *is* the marginal cost.

When there is competition, and this theory causes established companies to continue to use what they already have in place, they pay far more than the full cost—because the company loses its competitiveness.

As Henry Ford once put it, "If you need a machine and don't buy it, then you will ultimately find that you have paid for it and don't have it."

Thinking on a marginal basis can be very, very dangerous.

## An Unending Stream of Extenuating Circumstances

This marginal-cost argument applies the same way in choosing right and wrong: it addresses the third question I discuss with my students, of how to live a life of integrity—and stay out of jail. The marginal cost of doing something "just this once" always seems to be negligible, but the full cost will typically be *much* higher. Yet unconsciously, we will naturally employ the marginal-cost doctrine in our personal lives. A voice in our head says, "Look, I know that as a general rule, most people shouldn't do this. But in this particular extenuating circumstance, just this once, it's okay." And the voice in our head seems to be right; the price of doing something wrong "just this once" usually appears alluringly low. It suckers you in, and you don't see where that path is ultimately headed or the full cost that the choice entails.

Recent years have offered plenty of examples of people who were extremely well-respected by their colleagues and peers falling from grace because they made this mistake. The political arena is littered with examples of people at the top of their game getting caught doing something that would never have crossed their minds when they first decided they wanted to serve their country. Insider-trading scandals have rocked nearly every generation of Wall Street titans. Scores of athletes, who had been worshipped by youngsters all over the world, have been caught abusing steroids or exhibiting scandalous personal behavior, sometimes losing their entire careers as a result. Olympic champions have been stripped of their titles, their medals returned. Reporters for major national newspapers have been caught outrageously fabricating details in articles, amid high expectations and deadline pressures to get great stories. All of those people surely began their careers with a true passion for what they were doing. No rising young athlete imagines that he or she will need to find ways to cheat to stay on top. Athletes believe they can work hard enough to earn their success. But then they are faced with that first opportunity to try something that might help them get an edge.

Just this once . . .

Nick Leeson, the twenty-six-year-old trader who famously brought down British merchant bank Barings in 1995 after racking up $1.3 billion in trading losses before being detected, suffered exactly this fate and talks eloquently about how marginal thinking led him down an inconceivable path. In hindsight, it all started with one small step: a relatively small error. But he didn't want to admit to it. Instead, he covered it up by hiding the loss in a little-scrutinized trading account.

It led him deeper and deeper down a path of deception. He made a series of bets in order to pay the losses back—but rather than paying off, they made the problem worse. He lied to cover lies; he forged documents, misled auditors, and made false statements to try to hide his mounting losses.

Eventually, he arrived at his moment of reckoning. He was arrested at the airport in Germany, having fled his home in Singapore. As Barings realized the extent of Leeson's debt, it was forced to declare bankruptcy. The bank was sold to ING for just 1 pound. Twelve hundred employees lost their jobs, some of them his friends. And Leeson was sentenced to six and a half years in a Singaporean prison.

How could hiding one mistake from his bosses end up leading to the undoing of a 233-year-old merchant bank, a conviction and imprisonment for fraud, and ultimately the failure of his marriage? It's almost impossible to see where Leeson would end up from the vantage point of where he started—but that's the danger of marginal thinking.

"The thing that I wanted . . . was success," he told the BBC. His motivation was not, he said, to get rich, but to continue to be seen as a success. When his first trading mistake threatened that perception, he started down the path that was going to lead him all the way to a Singaporean jail cell. He had no way of knowing that's where it was going to end, but as soon as he took that first step, there was no longer a boundary where it suddenly made sense to turn around. The next step is always a small one, and given what you've already done, why stop now? Leeson described the feeling of walking down this dark road: "[I] wanted to shout from the rooftops . . . this is what the situation is, there are massive losses, I want it to stop. But for some reason you're unable to do it."

That is the peril of marginal thinking, of doing something just this once, of only applying your rules most of the time. You can't. I'm sure Leeson could have imagined the consequences of owning up to his initial mistake, painful though they might have been. The costs of taking the high road are always clear like that. But the costs of taking the low road—the one Leeson took—don't seem that bad at the start. There is no way Leeson could have imagined that covering up that one small mistake would result in his losing everything he valued in his life—his freedom, his marriage, and his career. But that's exactly what ended up happening.

## 100 Percent of the Time Is Easier Than 98 Percent of the Time

Many of us have convinced ourselves that we are able to break our own personal rules "just this once." In our minds, we can justify these small choices. None of those things, when they first happen, feels like a life-changing decision. The marginal costs are almost always low. But each of those decisions can roll up into a much bigger picture, turning you into the kind of person you never wanted to be. That instinct to just use the marginal costs hides from us the true cost of our actions.

The first step down that path is taken with a small decision. You justify all the small decisions that lead up to the big one and then you get to the big one and it doesn't seem so enormous anymore. You don't realize the road you are on until you look up and see you've arrived at a destination you would have once considered unthinkable.

I came to understand the potential damage of "just this once" in my own life when I was in England, playing on my university's varsity basketball team. It was a fantastic experience; I became close friends with everyone on the team. We killed ourselves all season, and our hard work paid off—we made it all the way to the finals of the British equivalent of the NCAA tournament.

But then I learned that the championship game was scheduled to be played on a Sunday. This was a problem.

At age sixteen, I had made a personal commitment to God that I would never play ball on Sunday because it is our Sabbath. So I went to the coach before the tournament finals and explained my situation. He was incredulous. "I don't know what you believe," he said to me, "but I believe that God will understand." My teammates were stunned, too. I was the starting center and to make things more difficult, the backup center had dislocated his shoulder in the semifinal game. Every one of the guys on the team came to me and said, "You've got to play. Can't you break the rule, just this one time?"

It was a difficult decision to make. The team would suffer without me. The guys on the team were my best friends. We'd been dreaming about this all year.

I'm a deeply religious man, so I went away to pray about what I should do. As I knelt to pray, I got a very clear feeling that I needed to keep my commitment. So I told the coach that I wasn't able to play in the championship game.

In so many ways, that was a small decision—involving one of several thousand Sundays in my life. In theory, surely I could have crossed over the line just that one time and then not done it again. But looking back on it, I realize that resisting the temptation of "in this one extenuating circumstance, just this once, it's okay" has proved to be one of the most important decisions of my life. Why? Because life is just one unending stream of extenuating circumstances. Had I crossed the line that one time, I would have done it over and over and over in the years that followed.

And it turned out that my teammates didn't need me. They won the game anyway.

If you give in to "just this once," based on a marginal-cost analysis, you'll regret where you end up. That's the lesson I learned: it's easier to hold to your principles 100 percent of the time than it is to hold to them 98 percent of the time. The boundary—your personal moral line—is powerful, because you don't cross it; if you have justified doing it once, there's nothing to stop you doing it again.

Decide what you stand for. And then stand for it all the time.

~

*When a company is faced with making an investment in future innovation, it usually crunches the numbers to decide what to do from the perspective of its existing operations. Based on how those numbers play out, it may decide to forgo the investment if the marginal upside is not worth the marginal cost of undertaking the investment. But there's a big mistake buried in that thinking.*

*And that's the trap of marginal thinking. You can see the immediate costs of investing, but it's really hard to accurately see the costs of not investing. When you decide that the upside of investing in the new product isn't substantial enough while you still have a perfectly acceptable existing product, you aren't* taking into account a future in which somebody else brings the new product to market. You're assuming everything else—specifically, the money you make on the old product—will continue forever exactly as it has up until now. A company may not see any consequences of that decision for some time. It might not get "caught" in the short term if a competitor doesn't get ahead. But the company that makes all its decisions through this marginal-costs lens will, eventually, pay the price. So often this is what causes successful companies to keep from investing in their future and, ultimately, to fail.

The same is true of people, too.

The only way to avoid the consequences of uncomfortable moral concessions in your life is to never start making them in the first place. When the first step down that path presents itself, turn around and walk the other way.

# EPILOGUE

~

*That business purpose and business mission are so rarely given adequate thought is perhaps the most important cause of business frustration and failure.*

—Peter F. Drucker

## The Importance of Purpose

A few weeks before the end of the fall semester in 2009, I learned that I had a cancer similar to the one that had killed my dad. I shared the news with my students, including the fact that my cancer might not respond to the therapies that were available. For several years, I'd used my last class to discuss with my students the same questions about their lives that I've posed for you in this book. Try as I might, however, my sense was that previously at best half of my students had left this class with a serious intent to change. The rest left with an assurance that the topics were relevant to other people, not to them.

For that class, that day in 2009, I wanted all of them. I wanted them to *feel* how important it was to think about the lives before them. As we discussed together the theories as applied to their lives and mine, our conversation was, indeed, more powerful than it had ever been before.

The reason, I think, is that we took time in the class to discuss how critical it is to articulate the purpose of our lives.

Whether they want one or not, every company has a purpose—it rests in the priorities of the company, and effectively shapes the rules by which managers and employees decide what is most important in each unique situation. In many companies, the purpose has come through an *emergent* strategy entrance, in which certain powerful managers and employees believe that the company is there solely to help them, as individuals, achieve their personal ends—whatever those might be. For those people, the company essentially exists to be used. Enterprises with such *de facto* purposes usually fade away—and very quickly the company, its products, and its leaders are forgotten.

But if an organization has a clear and compelling purpose, its impact and legacy can be extraordinary. The purpose of the company will serve as a beacon, focusing employees' attention on what really matters. And that purpose will allow the company to outlive any one manager or employee. Apple, Disney, the KIPP Schools (chartered schools in inner-city neighborhoods that have remarkable results), and the Aravind Eye Hospital (an eye surgery hospital in India that serves more patients than any other eye hospital in the world) are examples of this.

Without a purpose, the value to executives of any business theory would be limited. Even though theory is able to predict the possible outcomes of an important decision, on what basis would the executives be deciding among them to determine which is the *best* outcome? For example, if I had presented my theory of disruption to Andy Grove and General Shelton without there being a clear understanding of the purpose of their respective organizations, I would have been little more than a facilitator of opinions. Purpose was the critical ingredient that guided them in the application of the theory.

In a similar way, to maximize the value of the advice in this book, you must have a purpose in your life. For that reason, I want to describe to you the best process I know to develop a purpose, and illustrate it with the example of how I used this process in my own life. Mine was a rigorous process, and I recommend it to you as well.

## The Three Parts of Purpose

A useful statement of purpose for a company needs three parts. The first is what I will call a *likeness*. By analogy, a master painter often will create a pencil likeness that he has seen in his mind, before he attempts to create it in oils. A likeness of a company is what the key leaders and employees want the enterprise to have become at the end of the path that they are on. The word *likeness* is important here, because it isn't something that employees will excitedly "discover" that the company has become at some point in the future. Rather, the likeness is what the managers and employees hope they will have actually built when they reach each critical milestone in their journey.

Second, for a purpose to be useful, employees and executives need to have a deep *commitment*—almost a conversion—to the likeness that they are trying to create. The purpose can't begin and end on paper. Because issues demanding answers about priorities will repeatedly emerge in unpredictable ways, employees without this deep conversion will find that the world will compromise the likeness by wave after wave of extenuating circumstances.

The third part of a company's purpose is one or a few *metrics* by which managers and employees can measure their progress. These metrics enable everyone associated with the enterprise to calibrate their work, keeping them moving together in a coherent way.

These three parts—likeness, commitment, and metrics—comprise a company's purpose. Companies that aspire to positive impact must never leave their purpose to chance. Worthy purposes rarely emerge inadvertently; the world is too full of mirage, paradox, and uncertainty to leave this to fate. Purpose must be *deliberately* conceived and chosen, and then pursued. When that is in place, however, then *how* the company gets there is typically emergent—as opportunities and challenges emerge and are pursued. The greatest corporate leaders are conscious of the power of purpose in helping their companies make their mark on the world.

The same is true for leaders outside of the business sphere, too. People who have led movements for change, such as Mahatma Gandhi, Martin Luther King, and the Dalai Lama, have had an extraordinarily clear sense of purpose. So, too, have social organizations that have fought to make the world a better place, such as Médecins Sans Frontiers, the World Wildlife Fund, and Amnesty International.

But the world did not "deliver" a cogent and rewarding purpose to them. And, unfortunately, it won't "deliver" one to you, either. The type of person you want to become—*what* the purpose of your life is—is too important to leave to chance. It needs to be deliberately conceived, chosen, and managed. The opportunities and challenges in your life that allow you to become that person will, by their very nature, be emergent.

I have a deep respect for the emergent process by which strategy coalesces—and, as a consequence, *how* I have pursued my purpose has evolved, step by step. Sometimes unanticipated crises and opportunities have felt like a wind at my back as I have worked toward my purpose. At other times they have felt like a numbing wind in my face. I'm glad that I wasn't too rigid in *how* I could achieve my purpose.

I have tried to define the purpose of my life, and I have helped quite a few friends and former students do this for themselves. Understanding the three parts composing the purpose of my life—a likeness, a commitment, and a metric— is the most reliable way I know of to define for yourself what your purpose is, and to live it in your life every day.

Finally, please remember that this is a process, not an event. It took me years to fully understand my own purpose. But the journey has been worthwhile. With that as background, I will share how I have come to understand my purpose.

## The Person I Want to Become

The likeness—the person I want to become—was the simplest of the three parts, and was largely an intellectual process.

The starting point for me—as it will be for most of us—was my family. I was very much the beneficiary of strong family values, priorities, and culture. I was born into a wonderful family, and as I grew up, my parents had deep faith. Their example and encouragement were powerful. They planted the seed of faith within me. It was not until I was twenty-four, however, that I came to know these things for myself.

These two parts of my life were a very rich source of inspiration for me of my likeness. I have used what I learned from my family, and from scriptures and prayer, to understand the kind of person I want to become—which, to me, also entails the kind of person God wants me to become.

Finally, I am a professional man. I genuinely believe that management is among the most noble of professions if it's practiced well. No other occupation offers more ways to help others learn and grow, take responsibility and be recognized for achievement, and contribute to the success of a team. I drew heavily upon this learning to mold my likeness.

From these parts of my life, I distilled the likeness of what I wanted to become:

- *A man who is dedicated to helping improve the lives of other people*
- *A kind, honest, forgiving, and selfless husband, father, and friend*
- *A man who just doesn't just believe* in *God, but who believes God*

I recognize that many of us might come to similar conclusions, whether based on religious beliefs or not, about the likeness we aspire to. It's a form of setting goals for yourself— the most important ones you'll ever set. But the likeness you draw will only have value to you if you create it for yourself.

## Becoming Committed

It is one thing to have these aspirations in mind. How do you become so deeply committed to these things that they guide what you prioritize on a daily basis—to drive what you will do, and what you will not do?

When I was in my twenties, the Rhodes Trust gave me an extraordinary opportunity to study at Oxford University in England. After I had lived there for a few weeks, it became clear to me that adhering to my religious beliefs in that environment was going to be *very* inconvenient. I decided, as a result, that the time had come for me to learn for certain and for *myself* whether what I had sketched out as a likeness—the person I wanted to become—was actually who God wanted me to be.

Accordingly, I reserved the time from eleven p.m. until midnight, every night, to read the scriptures, to pray, and to reflect about these things in the chair next to the heater in my chilly room at the Queen's College. I explained to God that I needed to know whether the things that I was holding in my hands were true—and what they implied for the purpose of my life. I promised that if He would answer this question, I would commit my life to fulfilling that purpose. I also said that if they weren't true, that I needed to know that, too—because then I would commit my life to finding what is true.

I would then sit in my chair, read a chapter, and then think about it. Was this actually true? And what did it imply for my life? I would then kneel in prayer—asking the same questions, and making the same commitments.

Each of us may have a different process for committing to our likeness. But what is universal is that your intent must be to answer this question: who do I truly want to become?

If you begin to feel that the likeness you have sketched out for yourself is not right—that this is not the person you want to become—then you must revisit your likeness. But if it becomes clear that it *is* the person you want to become, then you must devote your life to becoming that person.

I can recall with perfect clarity the intensity with which I focused on seeking to know if my likeness was right—and then committing to it. It is this intensity that truly makes this valuable—it becomes the oil brush strokes that powerfully replicate on canvas what starts as the pencil draft on paper.

As I followed this process, it became clear to me through feelings that I sensed in my heart and words that came into my mind that I had my likeness correct. It confirmed for me that the characteristics I sketched—kindness, honesty, being a forgiving and selfless person—were the right ones. I saw in my likeness a clarity and magnitude that I had never conceived before. It truly changed my heart and my life.

For me, defining the likeness of the person I wanted to become was straightforward. However, being deeply committed to actually becoming this type of person was hard. Every hour I spent doing that while at Oxford, I wasn't studying applied econometrics. At the time, I was conflicted about whether I could really afford to take that time away from my studies, but I stuck with it.

Had I instead spent that hour each day learning the latest techniques for mastering the problems of autocorrelation in regression analysis, I would have badly misspent my life. I apply the tools of econometrics a few times a year, but I apply my knowledge of the purpose of my life every day. This is the most valuable, useful piece of knowledge that I have ever gained.

## Finding the Right Metric

The third part of my life's purpose was to understand the metric by which my life will be measured. For me, this took the longest. I didn't come to understand that until about fifteen years after the experience at Oxford.

I was driving to work early one morning when I got a sudden and very strong impression that I was going to receive an important new assignment from my church, which has no professional clergy and asks every member to shoulder important duties. A couple of weeks later I learned that a particular church leader in the area was going to leave. I put two and two together and concluded that this was the opportunity that I received the impression about.

But that's not what happened. I learned that another man was asked to serve in this position. I was just crushed—not because I had ever aspired to a hierarchical position, but because I always have aspired to play an important role in strengthening our church. Somehow I felt that if I had been given this role, I would have been in a position to do more good for more people than if I weren't in the role.

This threw me into a two-month period of crisis; I had believed I could have done a very good job.

As has been so often the case in the most difficult parts of my life, this personal confusion precipitated an insight that became the third element of my purpose—the metric by which my life will be measured. I realized that, constrained by the capacities of our minds, we cannot always see the big picture.

Let me explain in management terms: police chiefs need to look at the numbers of each type of crime, over time, to know whether their strategy is working. The manager of a business cannot see the complete health of the company by looking at specific orders from specific customers; he or she needs to have things aggregated as revenues, costs, and profits.

In short, we need to aggregate to help us see the big picture. This is far from an accurate way to measure things, but this is the best that we can do.

Because of this implicit need for aggregation, we develop a sense of hierarchy: people who preside over more people are more important than people who are leaders of fewer people. A CEO is more important than a general manager of a business unit; that general manager is more important than the director of sales; and so on.

Now let me explain in religious terms: I realized that God, in contrast to us, does not need the tools of statisticians or accountants. So far as I know, He has no organization charts. There is no need to aggregate anything beyond the level of an individual person in order to comprehend completely what is going on among humankind. His only measure of achievement is the individual.

Somehow, after all of this, I came to understand that while many of us might default to measuring our lives by summary statistics, such as number of people presided over, number of awards, or dollars accumulated in a bank, and so on, the only metrics that will truly matter to my life are the individuals whom I have been able to help, one by one, to become better people. When I have my interview with God, our conversation will focus on the individuals whose self-esteem I was able to strengthen, whose faith I was able to reinforce, and whose discomfort I was able to assuage—a doer of good, regardless of what assignment I had. These are the metrics that matter in measuring my life.

This realization, which occurred nearly fifteen years ago, guided me every day to seek opportunities to help people in ways tailored to their individual circumstances. My happiness and my sense of worth has been immeasurably improved as a result.

## The Most Important Thing You'll Ever Learn

As I have gone through life as a father, a husband, an executive, an entrepreneur, a citizen, and an academic, the knowledge of purpose that I have derived has been critical. Without it, how could I ever have known to put the important things first?

This was put into stark relief recently as I had to navigate one of the biggest challenges of my life. Almost immediately after I started writing this book with James and Karen, and in remission from cancer, I suffered an ischemic stroke. A clot lodged itself in the part of my brain where writing and speaking are formulated. It resulted in "expressive aphasia." I could not speak or write, beyond just a few simple words initially.

This was a hard one. My job as a professor is dependent on those faculties.

Since that day, I've been working to learn to speak again, one word at a time. Regaining my cognitive faculties and my speech was so demanding, and the progress was so discouragingly slow, that it absorbed nearly all of my time and energy. For the first time in my life, I became focused on myself and on my problems. It was a numbing, downward spiral—and for the first time in my life I truly felt despair. The more I focused on my problems, the less energy I had to get better.

I recognized that I had come to a fork in the road. I could try to hide my problems, retreat from the world, and focus on myself. Or I could change paths. I resolved that I needed to refocus on expending as much of my cognitive and physical capacity as possible on what I knew to be my purpose. And as I did that—focusing on resolving others' challenges rather than my own—the despair fled, and I felt happy again.

I promise my students that if they take the time to figure out their life's purpose, they'll look back on it as the most important thing they will ever have discovered. I warn them that their time at school might be the best time to reflect deeply on that question. Fast-paced careers, family responsibilities, and tangible rewards of success tend to swallow up time and perspective. They will just sail off from their time at school without a rudder and get buffeted in the very rough seas of life. In the long run, clarity about purpose will trump knowledge of activity-based costing, balanced scorecards, core competence, disruptive innovation, the four Ps, the five forces, and other key business theories we teach at Harvard.

What's true for them is true for you, too. If you take the time to figure out your purpose in life, I promise that you will look back on it as the most important thing you will have ever learned.

\* \* \*

I HAVE WRITTEN this book with my wonderful and capable coauthors to help you to be successful and happy in your career. We hope that it will help you find deep happiness in the intimate and loving relationships with members of your family and your friends—because you accord to them the investments of your time and your talent that they merit. We hope that this book will also bolster your resolve to conduct your life with integrity. But most of all, we hope that in the end, we all will be judged a success by the metric that matters most.

How will *you* measure your life?

# ACKNOWLEDGMENTS

~

Many business researchers, consultants, and writers create and sell us static views—snapshots—of technologies, companies, and markets. The snapshots describe at a specific point in time the characteristics and practices of successful companies versus struggling ones; or of executives who are performing better and of those who are not at the time of the snapshot. Explicitly or implicitly, they then assert that if you want to perform as well as the best-performing ones, you should follow what the best companies and the best executives do. The snapshots tell us about those that are ahead and behind in the race. But they tell us little about how they got there. Nor do they tell us what is likely to happen in the future to those in the snapshots.

My colleagues, my students, and I have eschewed the profession of photography. Instead we are making "movies" of management. These are not, however, typical movies that you might see at a theater, where you see fiction that was conceived in the minds of the producers and screenwriters. The unusual movies that we're making at Harvard are the "theories" that we summarize in this book. They describe what *causes* things to happen, and *why*. These theories compose the "plots" in these movies. In contrast to the movies in a theater that are filled with suspense and surprise, the plots of our movies are perfectly predictable. You can replace the actors in our movies—different people, companies, and industries—and watch the movie again. You can choose the actions that these actors take in the movie. Because the plots in these movies are grounded in theories of causality, however, the results of these actions are perfectly predictable.

Boring, you say? Probably to those who seek entertainment. But for managers who need to deliver results, the theories essentially allow them to run simulations, predicting the short- and long-term results of various actions. Because the theory is the plot, you can rewind the movie and repeatedly watch the past, if you want, to understand what causes what, and why, to this point. Another feature of movies of this sort is that you can watch the future, too—before it actually occurs. You can change your plans, based upon different situations in which you might find yourself, and watch in the movie what will happen as a result.

I am deeply indebted to many people who have helped me develop this body of theory that describes how the managers' world works. Professors Kent Bowen and Willy Shih taught me about what theory means, and how to use the scientific process to create powerful theories in the realm of social sciences. Their guidance in my research has been priceless.

My other teaching colleagues—Steve Kaufman, Ray Gilmartin, and Chet Huber; my MBA and doctoral students at Harvard and MIT; and the partners and members at Innosight and the Innosight Institute are some of the smartest and most selfless people in the world. Every day they use our theories to explore how to solve problems and create growth opportunities for companies. But they also find situations or outcomes that our research cannot yet explain, and they then help me resolve these anomalies and improve the theories. I never imagined that I would have this opportunity to work with people of this caliber. And I never imagined that my students could in fact be my teachers.

Many of those who write about how to find happiness in our families and our personal lives are plying the same types of snapshots—of successful people and happy families juxtaposed against unsuccessful and unhappy ones. They also prescribe simple bromides, promising that if you do the same things that they do, you'll be successful and happy, too. The paramount assertion of this book is that the theories that describe how management works also explain a lot about what causes success and happiness in families, marriages, and within ourselves—and what causes the opposite as well. This means that the theories, or "movies" that enable us to envision what the future holds in store for companies, can help us see the predictable results that come from choices and priorities we might make in our personal lives.

Many of these insights emerged in Sunday worship meetings with fellow members of the Church of Jesus Christ of Latter-Day Saints over the past decade across the northeastern quadrant of North America. It is hard to describe these meetings to those who have never experienced them. Their intellectual rigor is comparable to that which I experience at Harvard. But their spiritual insight is unmatched—so that we can learn things from the outside in, and from the inside out, about how our lives will be measured. I'm grateful for these wonderful friends, from whom I continue to learn so much about the truths of eternity.

I can't imagine how I could have found more capable colleagues than Karen Dillon and James Allworth to work as coauthors with me on this book. They patiently coaxed important but imprisoned insights from my brain as I have struggled to recover from my stroke. I invited them to join me because their perspectives on the world differ from my own. Even when I could be only a limited verbal contributor they somehow were able to lead balanced arguments and discussions among the three of us, representing my perspectives by proxy even when I couldn't cogently verbalize my concerns and contributions. James is one of the smartest of the thousands of students I have known at HBS over the last two decades. But he is a truly humble and selfless man. Karen is among the best writers and editors on earth; issue after issue, her craft was apparent on each page of the *Harvard Business Review*. I have made capable colleagues and lifelong friends through this process. I will never be able to thank them enough.

As my life has become complicated, I would have become a befuddled, absent-minded professor without Emily Snyder, and Lisa Stone before her. They have brought serenity, kindness, order, beauty, and fun to my world and to everyone they meet. My visitors typically leave feeling that meeting Emily or Lisa was the highlight of their visit. Clay is secondary.

My wife, Christine, and our children, Matthew, Ann, Michael, Spencer, and Katie, have questioned, tested, edited, and answered every paragraph of this book. And well they should, because the development and application of these ideas truly have been a family affair. When I fell in love with Christine I had seen a few snapshots about marriage and fatherhood. We and our children have now studied individually and collectively the movies that the theories in this book have given to us. It is quite stunning to see how accurately the plot in these movies has predicted the results from the actions that we have chosen. I am grateful beyond words for their courage in making the choices that have brought us such happiness. I dedicate this book to them—and hope that the thoughts in this book will help you, as they have helped us.

—*Clayton Christensen*

I MUST CONFESS: if you'd told me three years ago, just before I was to embark on an adventure to business school in a faraway land, that I was going to come out the other side as the coauthor of a book ... well, I almost certainly would not have believed you. If you had told me that it was going to be a book based upon applying some of the most rigorous business theories in the world to finding happiness and fulfillment in life ... well, in that case, I might have even laughed.

It is funny how life works out sometimes.

The starting point for my acknowledgments most certainly has to be someone whom I feel incredibly lucky to be able to call a mentor and a friend: Clay Christensen. I can tell you that the path my life was on changed the very first day that I sat in class with Clay. After warning us that he learned the most from the classes at school he found the most difficult, he cold-called me (this is business school–speak for the unexpected and often difficult question at the start of a class). In a scene to be played out many times after, he patiently waited as I fumbled my way through, and then very gently made sure that we all truly understood the answer to the question he had asked. Repeat this for a semester—learning from a teacher who has a genuine interest and concern for everyone in the classroom, and who just happens to be one of the smartest people in the world—and by the end, I promise you, you will have learned a lot. Everything Clay does is driven by that genuine interest and concern for those around him. In the entire time I have known him, I have never seen it waver. It was there partway through the semester, when he was diagnosed with cancer—as soon as he could, he was straight back in class with us. It was overwhelmingly powerful on our last day of class, when he worked through with us the three questions that are contained within this book. His family was in the room at the time; none of us had any idea whether it was the last time he would be able to take that class. The only effect it seemed to have on him was to make him even more determined to help us.

For the longest time, I wondered what I had done to deserve the privilege of being able to work with Clay. Part way through my time working with him, I came to realize that really, it wasn't about me at all. In the words of Goethe: "Treat people as if they were what they ought to be and you help them to become what they are capable of being." He might have let me *think* I was helping him, but in reality, it has always been he that was helping me.

Clay: I have learned so much from you. Short of my parents, you have done more to change the way I think about the world than anyone. Thank you so very much.

There is another person whom, in the course of this book, I have come to know very well and also now have the privilege of being able to call a good friend: Karen Dillon. When Karen and I first met, it was under circumstances in which I was looking for her help, but in which she had no real cause to help me. Her response? To aid me as much as she could, and then more. In the same way that my first interaction with Clay was to foreshadow our relationship, so, too, was it with Karen. She is someone who does nothing by half, is patient, selfless, has the most wonderful sense of humor, and man, is she wicked smart, too. I feel lucky not just to have met her, but to have had the chance to work with her. Whenever things started getting difficult, Karen would be the one who would drag us out again—with her smarts, with her humor, and with a boundless positive attitude. In fact, it's almost *fun* flying into the face of adversity with Karen around; not only do you know she has your back but you also know she'll pull you through.

Karen: you made this entire project a joy. There is no person I'd rather have in the trenches beside me than you.

Hollis Heimbouch, our publisher at HarperCollins. Hollis, thank you for having faith in this project, and for having faith in us. I know we didn't always make your life easy, but I have no doubt that your efforts have made this much more than it otherwise would ever have been.

Danny Stern, our agent. Danny, thank you, also, for believing in us. There are few people who engender a sense of trust as much as you; your frank and fearless advice has been so immensely helpful throughout this process.

There are a number of my colleagues who provided advice, feedback, and suggestions as we undertook this project: Wrede Petersmeyer, Max Wessel, Rob Wheeler, Rich Alton, Jason Orgill, and Lucia Tian. Thank you, guys. Your brilliance, humor, and patience not only made this better than it would have otherwise been, but you have no idea how important you were in keeping me sane in Morgan 130! I truly couldn't ask for a more wonderful group of people to work with.

Lisa Stone and Emily Snyder, who not only helped to keep us organized, but helped to keep us motivated. Lisa and Emily, you guys have no idea how much your boundless enthusiasm has helped when the path in front of us became difficult.

There are some folks in the class of 2010 at HBS to whom I owe thanks: Christina Wallace, whose idea it was for Clay to speak to our graduating class; and Patrick Chun and Scott Daubin, our class presidents, who took the idea and made it a reality. Many of us recognized that the message Clay shared with us in class that day deserved to be shared more widely; you guys had the vision and determination to do something about it.

I owe thanks to a number of my professors for their help and guidance at various stages of this process. Peter Olson, thank you for your mentorship and for your help in navigating the treacherous waters of the literary world. Your advice and encouragement was invaluable. Similarly, Anita Elberse—my whole frame of reference for the content industries came in large part from your class. Apologies for the numerous ambushes in the corridors, and thank you for so generously sharing your insight. Finally, Youngme Moon— thank you for your many and wonderful suggestions for the marketing of our efforts, and being so generous with your time in allowing me to bounce ideas off of you.

I want to thank my friends at Booz & Co. for their patience and support. Two people come to mind in particular:

Tim Jackson and Michele Huey. I doubt I would have made it here in the first place without your help. Thank you both.

There's a story that Clay tells in the second chapter about his classmates keeping each other honest, pushing one another to do something with their lives that they really felt was meaningful. I had a pretty broad grin on my face when I first heard that story, because although as students of Harvard Business School Clay and I are separated by a few years, I, too, had benefited from exactly the same thing. A group of my own friends pushed me, challenged me, cajoled me into doing something I believed in, something I thought was meaningful, and they wouldn't let me settle: Taahir Khamissa, Anthony Bangay, Gui Mercier, and D. J. DiDonna. Similarly, back home, Kamy Saeedi and John Smith played a very similar role. Thank you, guys, so much.

I need to thank the respective families of my two coauthors. This has been a labor of love for all of us, and I know the demands of this project have at times pulled your loved ones away from you. On top of that, we've asked you for edits and for feedback, we have interrupted everything from overseas moves to holidays, and we have even pulled some of you into the stories contained in these pages. For being the support crew that has kept us on track, Christine and Richard, you deserve particular thanks. It's been a joy getting to know you both.

And then, there is my own wonderful family. My parents, Mick and Susie, and my sister, Niki. I can state with absolute certainty that without your tireless help, support, and love . . . well, none of the many wonderful opportunities I have had—let alone this one—would have been open to me. I know how much you have sacrificed to make that so, and I know that I do not, and cannot, say thank you enough. It's been amazing to see how, as we've gone through this process of writing this book, you seem to have just intuitively applied so much of what's contained here to our own family. I owe you more thanks than I could ever hope to commit to paper.

And finally, I want to thank *you*—the person reading this right now. Thanks for having the trust in us to pick this up and listen to what we have to say. We have poured our hearts into this in the hope that we might be able to help you, and that would have been in vain were you not so generous to give us a chance to do so.

I truly, truly hope that you're able to get as much out of these pages as I did in helping to craft them.

—*James Allworth*

Meeting clayton christensen changed my life.

In the spring of 2010, as the editor of *Harvard Business Review* magazine, I had been casting around for an article that would add a little extra something to our summer 2010 double issue. I realized that the students about to graduate from Harvard Business School that spring had applied to business school when the economy was still rosy and everything seemed possible—but they were now graduating into a world of uncertainty. I reached out to Patrick Chun, copresident of the graduating HBS class, to pick his brain for ideas. It was Patrick who first told me that Christensen had been selected by the class to address them and that his words had been extraordinarily moving.

So I tracked Clay down and asked if I could come by his office to try to capture some of what he had told the students. He willingly obliged, and I traipsed over to campus with a digital recorder and the sole agenda of getting an article for my magazine.

When I walked into his office, I was thinking only about the lives of graduating MBA students. When I emerged an hour or so later, I was thinking about my own.

Every question Clay asked, every theory he discussed, resonated with me. As I've reviewed the transcript of our original conversation in the months since then, I can see the discussion peppered with my own evolving thoughts. Was I actually allocating my resources to the things that mattered most to me? Did I have a strategy for my life? Did I have a purpose? How would I measure my life?

I stood in the parking lot of HBS a few hours later and knew I didn't like my answers to those questions. Since then, I have changed almost everything about my life with the goal of refocusing around my family. I resigned from *Harvard Business Review* in the spring of 2011 with the good wishes of my colleagues and have spent the months since then balancing writing this book with Clay and James and being truly present in the moments of my own life—and more important, in the lives of my husband and daughters. I haven't regretted a single decision I've made since the day I first left Clay's office.

It's been an honor to work with my coauthors, Clay and James, on this book. This book is a reflection of many, many hours of discussion and debate among the three of us. I consider myself lucky to have had the invaluable benefit of a private tutorial in the theories of Clayton Christensen. But more important, I consider myself privileged to have had the chance to collaborate with a man who is brilliant, kind, and generous not some of the time, not much of the time, but *all* of the time.

And James. I couldn't possibly have imagined the journey we'd go on together when we first spoke back in the spring of 2010. Working with you forced me to raise my game in every possible way. I learned so much from you, not least how wonderful it is to have a true partner with whom to collaborate—and laugh along the way. You are one of the brightest and most decent people I've ever had the privilege to work with. For me, one of the best things to come out of this project is the wonderful friendship we have forged in the days, weeks, and months of working so closely on something that we cared so deeply about.

I'd like to thank my colleagues at *HBR* for their support of the original article (and my subsequent plans to recalibrate my life), notably HBR Group editor in chief, Adi Ignatius, who supported me and the idea of the article right from the start; executive editor Sarah Cliffe, whose wise counsel and suggestions improved everything I ever worked on; Susan Donovan, who polished the original article to perfection; Karen Player, who made sure the article was beautifully presented; Dana Lissy, who always allowed me to push the time and space boundaries for something worthwhile; Eric Hellweg, who made sure the article found its audience on HBR.org and has provided sage advice about the Web since then; Christine Jack, who constantly buoyed my spirits by being such a kind colleague; and Cathy Olofson, now at the Christensen-founded Innosight, who made sure the article got into all the right hands. Tina Silberman, thanks for being the perfect meeting partner. I know no one will ever come close to you! Jane Heifetz, thanks for keeping me laughing. The world needs more Janes. Clay's assistant in the spring of 2010, Lisa Stone, was wonderfully helpful in preparing the original article. Emily Snyder, Clay's current assistant, has been a real bright light: the source of ceaseless support throughout the writing of the book. Danny Stern and his team at Stern + Associates have offered steady guidance and encouragement throughout this process. Diane Coutu, I thank you for sharing your enthusiastic vision of reinventing your own life with me that one day we drove across town together. You have no idea what wonderful things you helped set in motion. To my friends, both inside and outside the workplace, you have been the source of so much joy and support over the years. I owe you all a debt of enormous gratitude.

I wanted to thank Skype, Google Docs, and Dropbox for making it possible to write this book with coauthors in Boston while living in London, but James tells me we should instead write a blog about how we used those tools to build our extraordinary working relationship. . . . So that will have to wait.

But most of all, I want to thank my family. My parents, Bill and Marilyn Dillon, who instinctively built the most wonderful, strong, and loving family culture I could possibly have hoped for. I consider it a life goal to be half the parents to my own children that they were to me. To my sister, Robin, and brother, Bill, I'm proud of the wonderful people you have become and even more proud to say that even after all these years, I still consider you both to be my closest friends.

And to my husband, Richard Perez, and my daughters, Rebecca and Emma, who endured dramatic changes in their own lives to support my work on this book and my quest to reset my life. You have provided support and inspiration in every way possible. I consider it a gift to be your wife and your mother. In you, I have discovered my purpose. I know how I will measure my life.

—*Karen Dillon*